ARCHITECTURE 06

ARCHITECTURE 06

THE GUIDE TO

THE RIBA AWARDS

TONY CHAPMAN

RIBA ✠ Trust

MERRELL
LONDON · NEW YORK

First published 2006 by Merrell Publishers Limited

Head office
81 Southwark Street
London SE1 0HX

New York office
49 West 24th Street, 8th Floor
New York, NY 10010

merrellpublishers.com

PUBLISHER Hugh Merrell
EDITORIAL DIRECTOR Julian Honer
US DIRECTOR Joan Brookbank
SALES AND MARKETING MANAGER Kim Cope
SALES AND MARKETING EXECUTIVE Amina Arab
SALES AND MARKETING ASSISTANT Abigail Coombs
ASSOCIATE MANAGER, US SALES AND MARKETING Elizabeth Choi
FOREIGN RIGHTS MANAGER Anne Le Moigne
MANAGING EDITOR Anthea Snow
PROJECT EDITORS Claire Chandler, Rosanna Fairhead
EDITOR Helen Miles
ART DIRECTOR Nicola Bailey
DESIGNER Paul Shinn
PICTURE RESEARCH MANAGER Liz Boyd
PRODUCTION MANAGER Michelle Draycott
PRODUCTION CONTROLLER Sadie Butler

British Library Cataloguing-in-Publication Data:
Architecture 06 : the guide to the RIBA awards
1.Architecture – Awards – Great Britain – Periodicals
2.Architecture – Europe – 21st century – Periodicals
I.Chapman, Tony II.Royal Institute of British Architects
720.7'941

ISBN-13: 978-1-8589-4342-8
ISBN-10: 1-8589-4342-6

Produced by Merrell Publishers
Edited by Tom Neville
Designed by Claudia Schenk
Printed and bound in Italy

CONTENTS

JUDGING
LUBETKIN

Stirling has a little brother: as it approaches its stroppy teens along comes the fledgling Lubetkin, mewling and puking. Having had the architectural prize world more or less to itself for a decade, save for the odd Pritzker, Royal Gold Medal and upstart Architect of the Year awards, now Stirling has the Lubetkin to give it a hard time. In practice, like all siblings born years apart, the two will have very little to do with each another. Stirling will continue to get all the best presents: a prestigious party venue, a £20k cheque from Auntie Isabel Allen, and guaranteed TV coverage from Uncle Kevin McCloud, while all Lubetkin gets is a (very nice) concrete trophy and a place at the RIBA Awards dinner. When it grows up maybe it will get its own ceremony and attract the attentions of the BBC (they are already prowling round it). For the time being it will have to make do with being the big fish in a pool of the minnows that are the RIBA Awards (but how quickly some of them grow up to be Stirling contenders).

Lubetkin was dreamed up by Paul Finch and myself on the 13.28 from Chelmsford, where we had been revisiting a rather good dentist's surgery, designed and practised in by the brother of my dentist – it's a long story and not the reason we gave it an award. But Paul and I had less parochial matters in mind that April morning in 2005. We were worrying about the integrity of the RIBA Awards, or, more precisely, about how to maintain more or less intact their unique selling point: that the panel visited every scheme. The moral ground was already shifting under us like tectonic plates in an earthquake. Despite the generosity of our sponsors, we could no longer visit all the entries we were getting from the EU. Only the previous week I had driven from Berlin to Prague in a day to see four buildings, only two of which we were even considering for an award (Zaha cheered me up en route though, or at least her BMW building did). Then there was the long weekend in Malta and Sicily seeing four more schemes, none of which had been shortlisted. I was exhausted. So were the Awards' finances: hence the moral ground shifting. The solution was to move the goalposts. 'What if –' an RIBA president suggested excitedly at a subsequent meeting – 'what if we call them RIBA European Awards? Then you can still say all the RIBA Awards entries have been visited. After all, you're not visiting the Worldwide entries ...' (as they were then called). I had to break it to him that we weren't visiting any of them. So, what if we visited a shortlist, then decided on a winner? Brilliant. What shall we call it? Lubetkin. But isn't he an overseas architect who came to the UK, not a UK architect working abroad? Pedantry. Like Stirling, it sounded right. We reckoned we were on to a winner. Now all we had to do was to find that winner.

South Africa and Canada – it sounds like a jolly but in fact it was a jolly long way in a jolly short time, money and time being synonymous for busy people. But at least it meant we were flying business class, thanks to Marley's millions. Marley, the tile and cladding people, had given the RIBA Awards an astonishingly generous endowment back in 1988, and we'd been living off the interest ever since. In the absence of a specific sponsor for these awards, it was time to dig deeper into the gold mine. And it could all have been a lot worse: two of the shortlist of three happened to be in the same country, even the same province. So we congregated in the BA executive lounge one Friday evening in May, looking and feeling anything but executive. Jack Pringle, the RIBA president, and closest to being a paid-up member of the jet set (he does part-own a Piper); Paul Finch representing media partners *The Architectural Review*, which he edits (and definitely not a *GQ* man); and Jeremy Till, chair of the Awards Group and professor of architecture at Sheffield, bedecked in check – the top half at least. Plus me, present to get them there and back more or less on time and to act as referee and cameraman.

Norman Foster, in a short BBC programme, chose the jumbo jet as his favourite building. His must have had a makeover, or perhaps upstairs in first class is very different. Business class consists of a series of interlocking clam-shells into which you slot yourself and try to sleep, or drink yourself into oblivion. I'd like to claim, as Jack did at the subsequent awards ceremony, that I too had slept with Paul Finch, but I scarcely had a wink on that twelve-hour flight.

The last time I was in South Africa the country was in a state of transition, and it still is, coming to terms with its apartheid past. One way is through commissioning a series of museums where people can come together to learn from the history of more than forty years of oppression. The Red Location Museum, named not for its political affiliations but after the colour of the rusting shacks that make up the township around it, is the first such museum to be built in such a location – in fact it is right next door to the site of the first positive act of rebellion against the apartheid regime, in 1952, when black workers walked through the entrance to New Brighton Station withouth showing their 'passes', saying to the police, 'Arrest us'. Which they did.

Jo Noero and his partner did two entries in the anonymous competition and came first and second. The challenge of the brief was to create a museum that could be read by illiterate people. It is a building full of symbolism, from the sawtooth roof that evokes the factories where trade-union opposition was fomented, to the rusting Cor-ten steel 'memory boxes' that recall the metal boxes migrant workers, away from their families for eleven months of the year, used to store their mementos of home.

This is a hugely flexible space: a tomb for heroes of the struggle and a place of memory. There is no prescribed route around the museum; rather, visitors move through the dim spaces between the towering memory boxes, where the present moves into the twilight of the past. Jo Noero is a hero of architecture in a country of only two thousand architects in a population of 44 million (compare this to the UK's thirty thousand architects in a population of 60 million). He is also a hero of the struggle. He wears his heart on his sleeve in a way British architects seldom do, and it suits him. His client, Rory Riordan, a civil-rights lawyer, is just as passionate. A white man who lived most of his life under apartheid and hated it, he risked his life speaking out against it and is still doing so, not least through his museum, lest the terrible mistakes should be repeated.

The following day was Sunday. Airlines being what they are, we had an enforced day of sightseeing in Cape Town, from the kilometre after kilometre of townships alongside the freeway to the airport, to the how-the-other-10-per-cent-lives in the still largely white suburbs. The townships are slowly being rebuilt, with electricity and sanitation, but it is a mammoth task, one that dwarfs the housing problems we think we have in south-east England.

Another overnight flight, another continent: North America via the briefest of touchdowns in Heathrow, and the old railway glories of the Fairmont Royal York Hotel, Toronto. Toronto has a somewhat interim feel to it. It has been described as New York designed by the Swiss, but if that were true it would be a whole lot tidier. Carved up by motorways, whole blocks are missing like gaps in the mouth of a chocaholic. Colonial-style houses survive cheek by jowl with tower blocks, all overseen by the soaring CN Tower, which we didn't get a chance to climb but from where I'm sure the city would look as though it had been properly masterplanned. As it is, it's all pretty loose-fit. We ambled through the quiet bank-holiday city – Torontonians were at home, doubtless busy celebrating Queen Victoria's birthday, something we haven't done for about a century. We stumbled on Will Alsop's Ontario College building – dubbed 'the dalmatian that swallowed a billiard table' – which we promptly wanted to call on to the Lubetkin shortlist, so clever is the way it clambers all over a mediocre building the planners would not allow the College to pull down. All criticism that it is out of context in this shabby rundown quarter is misplaced: there is no context. I'm afraid I wouldn't let them call it in as it won a Worldwide Award last year.

But the one we had come to see was even better. This was Stefan Behnisch's Terrence Donnelly Centre for Cellular and Biomolecular Research, part of the University of Toronto. When is an atrium not an atrium? When it is really a glazed-in gap between two buildings. The architects have cleverly borrowed the façade of the next-door building and made it the outer wall of a gigantic greenhouse, rising to twelve storeys, with bamboos reaching roughly halfway up (by now they're probably poking at the roof). We took the lift to the top floor and worked our way down in the engaging company of the director, Brenda Andrews. Spiral stairs link the upper floors, connecting the break-out areas at the end of each of the big open-plan labs. On the lower floors a more conventionally configured and rather grander staircase takes over, switchbacking down through the greenhouse to the first floor. Dr Andrews was immensely proud of her centre and claimed it had led to increased productivity, even if, as is often the case, breakthroughs depend more on serendipity than application. We sat on the benches, studying the façades: coloured panels on the longer elevation, fritted or plain glass on the others. It is the only sign of the architect's trademark exuberance that is so much in evidence in many of his other buildings, and nowhere more so than in his Dresden school, which really did reinvent a building type. That's still my favourite – and Stefan's too, he told me. He's a man whose pride in his buildings is plain, and a brilliant critic, as we discovered later in the year when he helped to judge Stirling.

The next day we were up early again to fly to Ottawa. It has the feel of an inorganic capital; too small for its own importance. It is said – by Canadians – that it's a nice place to live but you wouldn't want to visit it, not unless you had a penchant for Po-Mo. Or lawns: the place has more lawns than a whole episode of

Desperate Housewives. But our spirits were greatly lifted by the Canadian War Museum. Libeskind has broken the mould; he has recast the way we memorialize past suffering. His influence is clear here, as is that of Zaha Hadid. But the best move – the walk across the roof – is all these architects', Moriyama and Teshima with Griffiths Rankin Cook. Moriyama and Rankin are the names to remember here. Old friends, they pay one another elaborate but clearly genuine Old World courtesy, a commodity that survives here in the New World. They had a fierce client in Joe Guerts, the museum's director, who was confined to a wheelchair for our visit after a skiing accident. This in no way limited his passion for the building or his pride in the small victories won over the architects. 'Would you believe it, they wanted a concrete floor in the lobby? It was I who insisted on the green slate tiles', he told us as he charged about the place with us in his wake. His self-belief had survived a discovery that might have broken lesser men: heavy military exhibits cannot be dragged across this vast lobby floor for fear of cracking the slate. The architects are by no means triumphant; they are wistful rather than smug, like the serious architects they are. And anyway, overall, this is a magnificent achievement.

We repaired to Ottawa's Fairmont Hotel for tea to bat around thoughts on what the judges had seen during the previous three days. The RIBA is sometimes accused of running pointless awards where apples are compared with pears. But you don't have to be a pear grower to know a good pear when you see one, or even a good apple grower. Quality will out, whether it be manifest in a modest house extension or a national museum. It's all about how the architects have responded to the challenge and used the means at their disposal: site, budget, materials and so on. And that doesn't mean that big-budget schemes are marked down; rather, that the judging will be looking for signs of money well spent.

Having just three projects to choose from, unlike the Stirling judges' six, should have made things easier. However, while the Stirling judges find it relatively easy to lose two or three, the Lubetkin judges were hanging on like a proud father to his triplets. Eventually and reluctantly they agreed that the polished brilliance of Behnisch was not going to compete with the raw emotion expressed in concrete and even tempered steel. It was Ottawa versus New Brighton.

What they liked about the Red Location Museum was that here was an example of architecture that makes a difference, that can change people's lives for the better. It also tells a story, but you could say the same about the Canadian War Museum. In the end they decided that the Canadian scheme was more skilful than moving, and the prize went to South Africa.

These are early days for the Lubetkin Prize. Some of the early Stirling judging left something to be desired – owing to illness no architect judged the first one; another judge (no, not that one) preferred to fly himself in by private plane, hardly entering into the communal spirit of the thing. Even this year Stefan Behnisch was a late (and excellent) substitute. And there was the usual round of cancelled flights, bags lost or stolen, and unpopular hotels.

It has been suggested by one critic that instead of sending round judges next year to any of our awards, we might bang up the relevant architects in a *Big Brother*-style house and let them fight it out. That really would be a People's Choice. Instead of relying on the collective expertise and dedication of teams of architects and lay judges, we'd be throwing it open to the whims and prejudices of the voting British public. Or how about *Strictly Come Building,* in which members of the public are paired up with celebrity architects and they have five minutes in which to design a building and persuade a panel of planners that they should get to build it. Or we could – and stop me if I'm getting silly – invite people to nominate their most hated buildings and then we could blow them up … oh no, that one's been done.

So maybe not. Instead I think we'll stick with the system we've got, even if it is being constantly refined and improved. This year some regional judges hated it (and I understand why) when the Awards Group judges – entirely within the rules – overturned some of their recommendations. But every system needs its checks and balances. Had the original decision stood, one building on the Stirling shortlist would not have been visited by the regional jury. The tectonic plates have been kept under control for a little while longer: on the whole the system works. After all, it has given us another pretty good Stirling winner.

THE STIRLING PRIZE

IN ASSOCIATION WITH THE ARCHITECTS' JOURNAL

The RIBA Stirling Prize, now in its eleventh year, is for the sixth year sponsored by *The Architects' Journal*. It is awarded to the architects of the building thought to be the most significant of the year for the evolution of architecture and the built environment. It is the UK's richest and most prestigious architectural prize. The winners receive a cheque for £20,000 and a trophy, which they hold for one year.

The prize is named after the architect Sir James Stirling (1926–1992), one of the most important British architects of his generation and a progressive thinker and designer throughout his career. He is best known for his Leicester University Engineering Building (1959–63), the Staatsgalerie in Stuttgart (1977–84) and his posthumous Number One Poultry building in London. His former partner, Michael Wilford, won the 1997 Stirling Prize for the jointly designed Stuttgart Music School, and in 2003 won an RIBA Award for the History Museum that completed Stirling's masterplan for the Stuttgart Staatsgalerie complex.

This year's Stirling assessors were Ian Ritchie (chair), Isabel Allen, Stefan Behnisch, Mariella Frostrup and Martha Schwartz.

The winner of the 2006 RIBA Stirling Prize in association with *The Architects' Journal* was the NEW AREA TERMINAL. BARAJAS AIRPORT. MADRID.

NEW AREA TERMINAL, BARAJAS AIRPORT .MADRID, SPAIN .RICHARD ROGERS PARTNERSHIP WITH ESTUDIO LAMELA

Whether the airport is approached by air or by land, the scale and complexity of the task that has been tackled and achieved here cannot be overestimated. What impresses is not only the extruded forms of the 1.2-km-long terminal and its 1-km-long satellite, linked by underground train and with thirty-six and twenty-six stands respectively, handling up to 35 million passengers annually, but also the neat industrial aesthetic of the car park with its nine thousand spaces, and the integrated train and metro station in its cathedral-like housing that will complete the development. After six years of construction the complex has doubled the capacity of the airport. It is also rapidly establishing Madrid as the gateway between South America and Europe, making it a southern European hub to rival Heathrow and Amsterdam further north.

To work effectively at this scale and with the unique complexity inherent in this building type, any potential solution must begin with a strong diagram linked to a powerful design concept. It was the clarity, legibility and drama of this combination in RRP's proposal that won an international competition in 1997; these have been carried through all stages of the design development.

In response to the key challenge, that of efficiently processing constantly changing passenger flows and the associated luggage handling, the building presents a straightforward linear diagram: a clear sequence of spectacular spaces for departing and arriving passengers. The various stages in the horizontal progression from arrival through check-in and passport/security to departure lounges and finally to aircraft are articulated by means of 'floating' parallel linear floorplanes, separated from each other by dramatic voids or natural light-filled 'canyons' spanned by bridges. They culminate in long views out through the fully glazed façade to the mountains beyond. Accommodation is, however, spread over six floors, with departure and arrival separated vertically. Three floors above ground deal with check-in, security, boarding and baggage reclaim; three floors below ground deal with maintenance, baggage processing and transferring passengers between buildings.

CLIENT AENA
STRUCTURAL ENGINEERS ANTHONY HUNT ASSOCIATES/TPS WITH OTEP/HCA
FAÇADE ENGINEER ARUP
QS HANSCOMBE LTD/GABINETE
CONTRACTORS UTE (TERMINAL AND SATELLITE)/DRAGADOS (CAR PARK)/ SIEMENS DEMATIC (BAGGAGE HANDLING)
CONTRACT VALUE £1238 MILLION
DATE OF OCCUPATION FEBRUARY 2006
GROSS INTERNAL AREA 760 MILLION SQUARE METRES
PHOTOGRAPHERS MANUEL RENAU (PAGES 14, 18, 19 CENTRE)/ROLAND HALBE (PAGE 15)/AMPARO GARRIDO (PAGE 19 TOP AND BOTTOM)

Graduated colour is used not, as in most Rogers schemes, to delineate services, but for wayfinding – your boarding pass will be marked with a colour and your route is instantly apparent as red gives way to orange, orange to yellow, yellow to green, green to blue. The device is carried through to the external structure, giving the whole building a joyful but never wilful exuberance. Elsewhere a restrained and functional approach is consistently applied to great effect, resulting in a visually clean, remarkably uncluttered and soothing environment.

The movement across floorplates is further promoted by the powerful wave form of the elegant oversailing roof. This unifying device succeeds in being both dominant and yet calmly and self-assuredly understated. The sinuous, lightweight consistency of the bamboo-slatted lining contrasts with the modular repetition of the gymnastic steel roof structure, which is in turn supported off a monumental concrete frame. The structure accommodates vast rooflights that provide shaded daylight throughout the upper level. Intentionally expressive air-conditioning outlets resembling giant barcode readers animate the baggage-collection stands.

The building is robust enough to withstand the results of minor battles lost in terms of signage and shopping, the simplicity and clarity of the architectural ambition being dominant. Nowhere is this more evident than on the outside, where the now aluminium-clad roof again emerges as the defining feature, sweeping across the building, minimizing its impact by means of the overhanging long edges and recessed clear glazed façades, cloaking the richness within and reinforcing the extruded nature of this infinitely extendable tour de force.

18 .THE STIRLING PRIZE WINNER

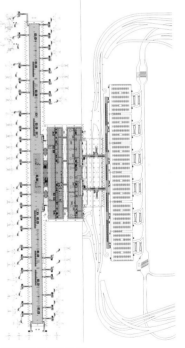

GROUND-FLOOR PLAN

BRICK HOUSE
.LONDON W2 .CARUSO ST JOHN ARCHITECTS

This new house is on an awkward back-land site that is shaped like a horse's head, and is overlooked by taller houses on three sides. Planning restrictions dictated what is effectively a single-storey-above-ground building, so as not to steal their daylight. The new house is accessed through an entrance at the end of a west London Victorian street and via a modern, austere, rendered corridor that forms the gently rising route to the house. The very limited palette of brick and concrete has been carefully detailed to create an outstanding piece of modern architecture. The result is a tribute to the determination of both architect and client.

This is a brave, intelligent and original study in the use of ordinary materials, developed in both a simple and a sculptural way. The concrete used in the ceiling is raw and coarse; where most architects would have chosen a smooth, creamy mix for an exposed soffit in a domestic setting, Caruso St John have gone for a concrete that is definitely more Queen Elizabeth Hall than Royal National Theatre. Further, the bold fractal geometries of the ceiling on the upper floor might seem gestural to some given that domestic context, but the varied heights and angles help to define the functional use of the spaces beneath them: a lower horizontal ceiling over the dining area, a high domed profile over the main sitting area. Minimal lighting is used to the same effect, with the architects having specified the freestanding uplighters as well as the fitted fixtures. They are also recommending pieces of furniture appropriate to the spaces.

This is a slow labour of love for the owners, so what the visitor sees is a work in progress rather than the quick-fit solution more appropriate to an upmarket developer's show-home, which is so often the case in houses with part-absentee owners. What is more, this is clearly what the client wanted: a large, single-volume living space for a family that spends much of its time in New York but wanted a London base that was right in the heart of things (hence the choice of the twenty-four-hour café culture of Notting Hill). It provides a massive contrast with their previous traditional London town house. That clambered inefficiently over five floors, meaning that younger family members

CLIENT PRIVATE
STRUCTURAL ENGINEER PRICE & MYERS
SERVICES ENGINEER MENDICK WARING
QS AND PLANNING SUPERVISOR JACKSON COLES
CONTRACTOR HARRIS CALNAN CONSTRUCTION
CONTRACT VALUE CONFIDENTIAL
DATE OF COMPLETION MAY 2005
GROSS INTERNAL AREA 380 SQUARE METRES
PHOTOGRAPHERS IOANA MARINESCU (PAGES 21, 23 TOP AND BOTTOM LEFT)/HÉLÈNE BINET (PAGES 22, 23 BOTTOM CENTRE)

ALSO SHORTLISTED FOR THE MANSER MEDAL

could be lost for hours (perhaps not an unpopular arrangement with the young people themselves). In the Brick House, all the bedrooms are at lower-ground level overlooking small (and currently bare) courtyard gardens that complete the geometry of the rooms they serve. In fact the shape of the site has informed the shapes of all the rooms – one bedroom is triangular. The main living space, incorporating dining and kitchen areas in one volume, and a separate study-cum-TV room occupy the upper floor, which is at raised ground-floor level. The varying planes of the interiors have a warmth and subtlety to them; the use of light is masterful.

Externally, it reads as a different house altogether, partly because of the site but partly because the skin gives no clue to the innovation within. The use of a single material, brick, in which to wrap the house is masterful and all but inevitable. While it was possible to pour in-situ concrete for the roof, it would have been nearly impossible to introduce the plant necessary to construct all the walls in a similar manner. And the eponymous bricks are just right, their pale terracotta colour and their recycled look (in fact they are all new) giving the house its character. While the bricks themselves appear to twist, it is only their positioning and the amount of mortar used that gives the illusion. Sadly, the Westminster planners insisted on a liverish brick for the courtyard walls as being more in keeping with ... with what, one wonders, as this is a street of stucco. The resulting discontinuity between inside and out is a rare disappointment in an otherwise immaculate house.

The architects have likened their house, hidden away behind a Victorian façade, to a Baroque chapel locked up behind a Roman street. This is by no means a fanciful conceit.

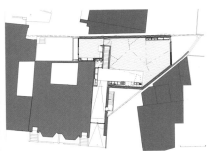

FIRST-FLOOR PLAN

23 .THE STIRLING PRIZE

EVELINA CHILDREN'S HOSPITAL .LONDON SE1 .HOPKINS ARCHITECTS

Part of the developing plan for the St Thomas's Hospital campus, the Evelina Children's Hospital is a beacon of optimism. Hopkins won the job through an RIBA competition back in 1999; it has been well worth the wait. This is a hospital where the patient, not the institution, is given priority.

This is Hopkins's first hospital and it shows, but the practice's inexperience is by no means the constraint it might at first appear to be. It means that they are not hidebound by experience and the caution that can attend it, and they are free of the preconceptions of regular practitioners in the field. In fact their very innocence was one reason the client fell for their scheme. And they fulfilled the imaginative brief, which was to come up with 'a hospital that does not feel like a hospital'. They have rethought the building type, bringing to the process their experience of commercial and education buildings.

In particular, their expertise in workspace planning has stood them in good stead. Hospitals, like offices (or schools), need a mix of cellular and open-plan spaces: enclosed for operations (literally), and flexible spaces for casual interaction. But they have consulted the experts, too, in the form of healthcare planners RKW, as well as user groups, including children. The result is a surprisingly open building, not only in the guise of the gigantic conservatory, which is overlooked by the wards, but also in the wards themselves, which open internally on to a serpentine corridor.

An entrance on Lambeth Palace Road, reached by a wheelchair- and pram-friendly ramp, stands at one end of an internal street that is illuminated by shafts of light from a spectacular atrium. As the campus plan develops the street will lead to what will become the main entrance, connecting to the new spine route at the heart of the hospital.

While the building is impeccably organized, the emphasis of the design is on providing an environment in which children feel comfortable and relaxed. Here, the usual overbearing institutional atmosphere of a hospital is dispelled. It is easy to find your way around the building. Wayfinding is fun rather than

CLIENT EVELINA CHILDREN'S HOSPITAL
STRUCTURAL ENGINEER BURO HAPPOLD
SERVICES ENGINEER HOARE LEA & PARTNERS
QS DAVIS LANGDON
CONTRACTOR M.J. GLEESON
CONTRACT VALUE £41.8 MILLION
DATE OF COMPLETION JANUARY 2006
GROSS INTERNAL AREA 16,500 SQUARE METRES
PHOTOGRAPHER PAUL TYAGI — VIEW

ALSO SHORTLISTED FOR THE RIBA INCLUSIVE DESIGN AWARD

patronizing: your appointment might be for Seashell Ward on Beach level, or you might be directed up to The Sky. Coloured pictograms are also a highly appropriate solution in a hospital in which 140 languages are used. Technical facilities, normally so associated with fear, are made pleasant and inviting; the shared play areas and the school are planned to be visible and enticing to newcomers and visitors; daylight reaches every hospital bed. Instead of the usual grim institutional corridors, a gently winding colourful path links the small wards. (Orthogonal geometries are reserved for the serious business of operating, intensive care and recovery that takes place on the floors beneath the atrium, though here, too, there is daylight.) The wards accommodate four or six children; a novel fold-down bed means a parent can sleep at the child's side. Overhead, the services are organized to allow the normal access ceiling to be replaced by a more domestic, child-friendly painted plaster.

The atrium is really a vast greenhouse the size of a football pitch. All it lacks is plants, though they were originally specified: the avenue of lemon trees would have made all the difference. But so, too, do the clowns, jugglers and musicians who turn up to entertain the children crowding into the space or watching from their ward windows. The only two permanent uses of this space are a café and a school, which is somewhat incongruously placed at one end, its rooms defined by screens. It looks almost like an afterthought, but staff insist its position boosts attendance, since the sicker children can look down on the classrooms and see what they are missing.

Evelina will not solve all the problems faced by the NHS in its massive building and refurbishment programme – it was largely funded by a charitable trust, which is how it could avoid the PFI route – but there are plenty of lessons here, not just for architects, but also for health administrators and politicians. And it was all delivered at a cost of £2550 per square metre, which is the going rate for a conventional NHS hospital and considerably less than a PFI-procured one at up to £3200 per square metre.

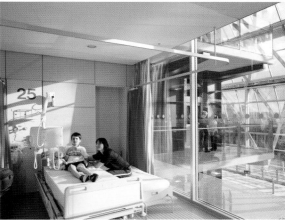

IDEA STORE WHITECHAPEL
.LONDON E1 .ADJAYE/ASSOCIATES

The idea of the Idea Store is to make the library a part of the community. The ivory tower has become one of glass, taking its scale from the nearby hospital, a sorting office and an old brewery. But its colourful character, a striped motif of green and blue glazed interlayers, echoes the awnings of the market stalls of the Whitechapel Road that press up against the building.

The Idea Store represents a new departure for public buildings. It is both civic and inclusive, iconic and contextual, but, most importantly of all, it is popular and loved by its users. Its civic character comes from its height and the boldness of a façade that hangs precariously over the pavement and those market stalls. Its inclusiveness comes from its situation right in the heart of the community it serves (figures show the profile of users directly matches that of the citizens of Tower Hamlets, with none of the expected bias towards those whose first language is English).

Customers can drop in on their way from Sainsbury's to the market. Two entrances welcome them into a ground floor that accommodates a familiar and unthreatening video store (more Blockbuster than bookstack) and a children's library. There was much discussion as to whether this or the café should be housed on the ground floor. In the end the clients and architects agreed to adopt the shopping-mall principle of an anchor store and use the café to draw people through the building and up to the top floor, of which half is given over to the café. This must be one of the best new public rooms in London, with stunning views towards the City: you have to be a banker or an insurance broker to do much better than this. Getting there, however, is complicated. A semi-external escalator shelters behind the suspended glazed front façade (which is set at a curiously jaunty angle to the building) and sweeps passers-by up to the facilities on the first and second floors. Sadly, value engineering saw to it that the escalator never reached the top as had been planned. But at least there are no entrance barriers or obstacles to getting into the heart of the building; instead, security is monitored by a series of friendly guards on each floor. This is a truly democratic building.

CLIENT LONDON BOROUGH OF TOWER HAMLETS
ENGINEER ARUP
GRAPHIC DESIGNER MODE
QS MILLER MITCHELL BURLEY LANE
CONTRACTOR WILLIAM VERRY
CONTRACT VALUE £12 MILLION
DATE OF COMPLETION SEPTEMBER 2005
GROSS INTERNAL AREA 3440 SQUARE METRES
PHOTOGRAPHERS LYNDON DOUGLAS (PAGES 29, 30 SOAR (PAGE 31)

WINNER OF THE RIBA INCLUSIVE DESIGN AWARD

In old money this is a library, but the 'idea store' label is more than an exercise in rebranding. It is an accurate representation of the building's mixed activities, which include nursery, dance studio, seminar spaces, internet facilities, a large external deck and physiotherapy training classrooms as well as the library itself.

The glazed façade is hung from deep timber mullions that support the shelving and accommodate seating and desk space. The interiors are also distinctive thanks to the careful placing and specification of the furniture and zigzag shelving, designed by the architects, and to the deep-red rubber floor. Exposed structural concrete fins in the ceiling act as a cool backdrop to the bespoke strip lighting, the design of which mirrors the patterns of the shelves. Detailing is carefully executed and robust, and is completely appropriate for such a heavily used building with a relatively small budget. Signage and graphics are fully integrated into the fabric in an inventive manner, with banks of squared-off lozenges indicating which floor you are on by dint of that floor's details standing proud of the others; and with the same information in Braille on their upper surfaces. It is the kind of solution (designed by Mode) you would have thought someone would have come up with before. No one has.

The building fully deserves its reputation both for its reinvention of a traditional type and for its architectural ambition. Most new libraries in this country are being procured through PFI, under which good design is often eroded or institutionalized. The Idea Store shows that ambitious clients picking adventurous architects and putting them to work in a traditional manner is still the best way to make good buildings.

GROUND-FLOOR PLAN

NATIONAL ASSEMBLY FOR WALES .CARDIFF .RICHARD ROGERS PARTNERSHIP

No one who saw the model for the competition-winning entry could forget its simple elegance: a Miesian glass box on top of a flight of steps leading up from the bay, under a wave-form roof – a minimalist pagoda. But this is Cardiff: nothing here is that simple. Comparison with the ill-fated Cardiff Opera House is both inevitable and salutary. Next door sits the upshot of a not dissimilar process: brilliant competition-winning scheme, loss of political nerve, architect sacked … but if Rogers's scheme was compromised, Zaha Hadid's was massacred. The Wales Millennium Centre is a popular if whimsical attempt at Welsh vernacular on a grand scale. Hadid's opera house would have been a piece of international architecture of the highest order.

Not least because the architects were reinstated, the Welsh National Assembly is still a remarkable achievement, all the more so as it was delivered within a design-and-build contract. For all its troubled history, this is an exceptional public building, and its democratic function is clearly expressed. From across the water, the debating chamber is revealed above the upper foyer space through fully glazed façades. Low slate walls define a series of accessible terraces linking the entrance with the boardwalk by the bay.

Already popular, the building clearly works on the many levels intended by its designers, with strong visual connections linking the building's context to the processes that go on inside. All this is reiterated by a confident and open internal organization. It is a delight to see children and parents peppered around the spectacular upper foyer under the flowing cedar-clad ceiling, enjoying the illusion that they are inside a beautifully honed musical instrument. This is the most impressive feature: precurved laths of Western red cedar are fixed over an angular steel frame, giving the building its organic character, both inside and externally on the soffit of the shade-giving canopy.

The many security measures added during the design process have inevitably affected the original clarity of vision, although the additions to the beautifully

CLIENT NATIONAL ASSEMBLY FOR WALES
STRUCTURAL ENGINEER ARUP
LANDSCAPE ARCHITECT GILLESPIES
ENVIRONMENTAL CONSULTANT BDSP PARTNERSHIP
PROJECT MANAGER SCHAL
COST CONSULTANT NORTHCROFT
CONTRACTOR TAYLOR WOODROW
CONTRACT VALUE £41 MILLION
DATE OF OCCUPATION FEBRUARY 2006
GROSS INTERNAL AREA 5308 SQUARE METRES
PHOTOGRAPHER RICHARD BRYANT – ARCAID

ALSO SHORTLISTED FOR THE RIBA SUSTAINABILITY AWARD

spare structural frame have been deftly handled. Not even the additional entrance box to one side detracts too much, and it does keep the main spaces free of the clutter of security. And once through those checks, visitors have the right to roam and take in the processes of government at work: to peek into the debating chamber or the committee and meeting rooms (all daylit by two canyons that run the length of the building); to take one of the 128 seats in the glazed-in public viewing gallery (twelve for wheelchair users) in the chamber; to have a coffee in the café bar at the oriel (upper) level; or simply to spend time in the vast lobby, taking in the views of the bay.

The circular debating chamber is at the heart of the building. A glazed lantern allows daylight to penetrate, while a roof cowl rotates with the wind to drive the natural ventilation. Internally, the roof sweeps up in a dramatic bell form, finished in concentric aluminium rings, with a glazed lantern above. A conical mirror suspended inside the lantern reflects more light into the chamber.

There has clearly been a strong desire from the team – matched by a revived political will – for the building to meet high environmental objectives, with the result that it has been awarded an excellent BREEAM rating, the best ever achieved in Wales. The materials were thoroughly reviewed in terms of their embodied energy and one-hundred-year-plus design life. Such techniques as biomass boilers, ground-source heat pumps and water harvesting are employed in a highly impressive way. This is a largely naturally ventilated building, with a mixed-mode system available to the debating chamber and public galleries, and the committee rooms. The system was not in use when the awards group visited and placed it on the shortlist; it was one of the hottest days of a hot summer and the building was comfortably cool throughout. A proper analysis of its systems and energy usage over a year and more should reveal exactly how much this building has to contribute to the great energy debate. It is likely to be a lot.

GROUND-FLOOR PLAN

PHAENO SCIENCE CENTER .WOLFSBURG, GERMANY .ZAHA HADID ARCHITECTS AND MAYER BÄHRLE FREIE ARCHITEKTEN BDA

'Phaeno' is a term relating to the idea of embodying or manifesting something, in this case scientific concepts – and even Zaha Hadid's soaring spaces struggle to compete for the attention of children of all ages with the scientific experiments and games that clutter the place. Here in 'Volkswagen City', however, the client has successfully commissioned a building that adds to our understanding of the subject.

For architects, this building is another kind of manifestation. It is the embodiment in the form of a major public project of work that many of us have only experienced in paintings, drawings and pavilions. It is fascinating to visit a building that is the realization of an imaginative world that we know vividly through twenty years of abstract images. Hadid has been pushing at the edges of architecture for a long time now, but until quite recently the experimentation has been done mainly on paper or screen. Now, in Strasbourg, Cincinnati, Leipzig and here in Wolfsburg, her extraordinary conceptions have been dragged into life. And if her offspring is sometimes more gawky than pretty, that is because some of Hadid's imaginings can be beyond the technical capabilities of mere mortals to deliver. For all that, this revolutionary building lets us experience space in ways that never seemed possible before.

The centre, the first of its kind in Germany, forms the full stop in a chain of culturally important buildings in the town by Scharoun, Aalto and Schweger. It is also a link on a route between the station (next door) and the new Volkswagen Town development. At first sight it is an object of mystery, a kind of undulating earthwork surmounted by a hovering frame. The paved surface of the town is plucked up like a tablecloth and turned into meandering, ramped routes through elevated exhibition spaces. There is an undercroft, a dark grotto carved out of looming dreamlike forms, like London's South Bank Centre only so much better.

Structural engineer Adams Kara Taylor was crucial to the realization of the scheme. The conical supports that raise the building off the ground and

CLIENT PHAENO SCIENCE CENTER
STRUCTURAL ENGINEERS ADAMS KARA TAYLOR (UK)/TOKARZ FREIRICHS LEIPOLD (GERMANY)
SERVICES ENGINEERS BURO HAPPOLD (BERLIN, LONDON)/NEK (GERMANY)
COST HANSCOMB GMBH
CONCRETE CONTRACTOR E. HEITKAMP GMBH
STEEL CONTRACTOR QUECK GMBH
CONTRACT VALUE € 40 MILLION
DATE OF COMPLETION NOVEMBER 2005
GROSS INTERNAL AREA 12,000 SQUARE METRES
PHOTOGRAPHERS HÉLÈNE BINET (PAGES 37, 39 CENTRE)/WERNER HUTHMACHER (PAGES 38, 39 TOP)/ RICHARD BRYANT – ARCAID (PAGE 39 BOTTOM)

create the undercroft required technical innovation. Instead of columns and beams, the dramatic result was achieved using self-compacting concrete. Phaeno is the largest building in Europe to have been created in this way.

The undercroft is perhaps the most successful part of the building. Hadid is surprisingly good at place-making. Another competition entry was an upside-down version of hers, taking the pedestrian routes over the roof (rather like the Canadian War Museum). Hadid's genius allied practicality and ambiguity, taking people on an ordinary journey from factory or sports arena to the town centre and luring them into a magical mystery tour. Doorways carved out of the concrete lead you up to an echoing barn full of gesticulating exhibits, mostly at child height. There is something of a mis-match between the architecture and its contents, but while exhibitions come and go, this architecture will remain and grow in our esteem.

There is action everywhere – and plenty of headroom. The architects describe the building as a visitation from a future warp-world. What is strange for the visitor is that it is weirdly reminiscent of many other buildings, all at once. The sensuous board-marked supports of Le Corbusier's Unité, a 1960s steel diagrid space-frame, a Baroque grotto. Even the windows look as though they might have been lifted from passing commuter trains. There is something almost Joycean in the babble of collaged constructional languages. The effect is that of a building that never settles down. It feels as though it is longing to become something else, and the sense of strain is palpable.

The point of a building like this is that it should be like a beacon, illuminating a possible future. It is at heart an experiment, at one moment swashbuckling, at another gangling. At its best it is primitive. It is possible to imagine the work of Zaha Hadid becoming more brutal and less willing to please. It is good to witness one of those rare moments when an architect and a client take great risks with a project, most of which have come off.

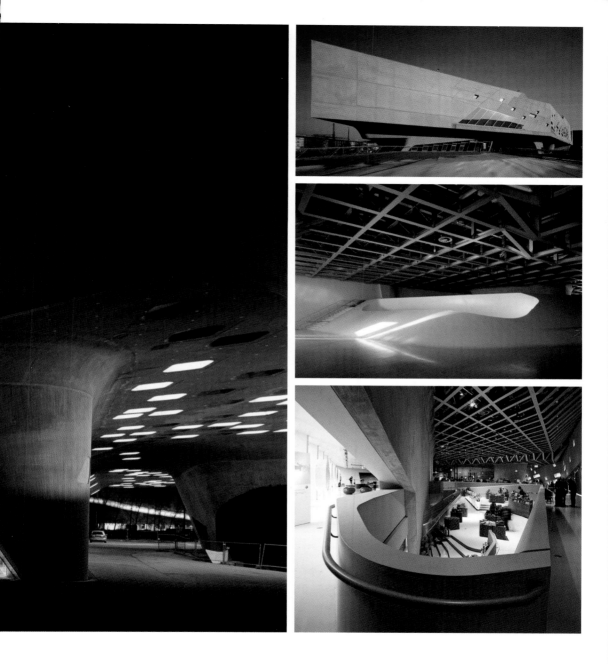

THE LUBETKIN PRIZE

This is the inaugural year of the RIBA Lubetkin Prize, an award given to the architect of the best building outside the EU by an RIBA member. The prize is named after the émigré architect from Georgia who came to Britain in the 1930s and went on to establish Tecton. He is best known for the two Highpoint buildings in Highgate, London, and for the Penguin Pool at London Zoo. The pool provided the inspiration for a cast-concrete plaque, designed and made by the artist Petr Weigl. This was presented at the RIBA Awards Dinner in June to the winner by Lubetkin's daughter Sasha, to fix inside their building.

The judges of the first RIBA Lubetkin Prize were RIBA president Jack Pringle, Professor Jeremy Till, chair of the Awards Group, and Paul Finch, editor of media partner *The Architectural Review*. They went to see a shortlist of three buildings that had already won RIBA International Awards in 2006: THE RED LOCATION MUSEUM OF THE PEOPLE'S STRUGGLE IN NEW BRIGHTON, BY NOERO WOLFF ARCHITECTS; THE TERRENCE DONNELLY BUILDING IN TORONTO, BY BEHNISCH ARCHITEKTEN WITH ARCHITECTS ALLIANCE; AND THE CANADIAN WAR MUSEUM IN OTTAWA, BY MORIYAMA AND TESHIMA/GRIFFITHS RANKIN COOK.

The winner was the RED LOCATION MUSEUM OF THE PEOPLE'S STRUGGLE.

RED LOCATION MUSEUM OF THE PEOPLE'S STRUGGLE .NEW BRIGHTON, SOUTH AFRICA .NOERO WOLFF ARCHITECTS

All museums are concerned with memory and history; it was singularly impressive to encounter one in which particular histories and memories have evoked an extraordinarily powerful architectural idea. The 'memory box', in which forced-migrant workers from the countryside carried artefacts to remind them of home, forms the basis for a building that is in itself one huge memory box. Designed in industrial form – with a sawtooth roof – because trade-union activity in factories provided impetus for the anti-apartheid struggle, the museum houses steel containers that themselves respond to the rusting steel shacks (hence 'Red Location') surrounding the site. The containers are tipped on end to make individual memory boxes, presenting curators with the equivalent of a blank canvas on which to exhibit memories, responses and ideas. The most powerful exhibition is a pile of box files containing the police records of people who were murdered, judicially or otherwise, during the struggle; above the files hang three ominous nooses. The building works as both metaphor and object: deliberately unglamorous, this is an architectural tour de force.

The oldest township in Port Elizabeth, where the first act of defiance occurred – when black and coloured railway workers refused to show their 'passes' to enter railway property – this is the most evocative of locations and symbolically significant for a museum of apartheid and its struggles. To build such a museum in the middle of the township that acted as a crucible for the struggle is an extraordinary achievement. The Red Location Museum rises to the challenge brilliantly, using architectural skill of the highest order to produce an unforgettable experience that is both viscerally and intellectually moving.

In accepting the award, architect Jo Noero made a speech that clearly moved and excited the audience at London's Hilton Hotel. The following version was written up by the architect after the event:

'It is a great honour to receive the Lubetkin Prize – the award means a lot to me particularly because Berthold Lubetkin has always been an architect whom

CLIENT RED LOCATION MUSEUM OF THE PEOPLE'S STRUGGLE
STRUCTURAL ENGINEER DE VILLIERS & HULME
QS WALTERS & SIMPSON
CONTRACTOR GROVE LOURENS
CONTRACT VALUE £2 MILLION
GROSS INTERNAL AREA 3600 SQUARE METRES
PHOTOGRAPHERS ROB DUKER (PAGES 46, 47)/DAVID SOUTHWOOD (PAGES 45, 48, 49)

I hold in the greatest regard. His work acts as an exemplar in reminding us about the power of architecture not only to move one but also to hold out the possibility of being able to make the world a better place in which to live.

'I practise in South Africa at a very interesting time in its history. The role of architecture has never been more critical in the country's history inasmuch as the transformation in which we are engaged is as much directed to equalizing opportunity and redistributing resources more equitably as it is directed to transforming our cities and the spaces within these cities physically – architecture has a huge role to play in achieving these ends. I would venture to say that the kind of architecture that is taught and practised in the country still holds to the now-unfashionable view that there is a fundamental relationship between purpose and form. I look upon the world of current architectural production sometimes with bemusement but mostly with rage and anger. The cynical manner in which architects today engage in making form to either brand, market or promote themselves more often than not at the expense of use and context is nauseating. In this regard the example of Lubetkin serves as a salutary reminder to us about how low we have sunk in the last twenty years or so …

'South Africa still holds a possibility for architecture to rehabilitate itself, since the process of transformation and reconstruction requires an engagement on the part of architects and planners to assist in this process. This is an area where huge opportunities exist. It is indisputable that we are building supermarkets and casinos like everywhere else; however, we are also building houses, schools, clinics and community centres for the urban poor. This massive infrastructural project of the state requires an intellectual engagement from architects where the form-making potential of the architecture demands the possibility of social transformation for the recipients. Surely this is what architecture needs to be. Not the insipid forms of social building projects funded by gambling that pander to market forces and that seek to commodify and reify through architectural form-making intrinsic human needs and desires.'

GROUND-FLOOR PLAN

46 .THE LUBETKIN PRIZE

47 .THE LUBETKIN PRIZE

CANADIAN WAR MUSEUM
.OTTAWA, CANADA .MORIYAMA AND TESHIMA/
GRIFFITHS RANKIN COOK

The Canadian War Museum is the result of a joint venture between two long-established father–son practices, one in Toronto, the other in Ottawa – and a strong, determined client. The design hand of septuagenarian Canadian Japanese architect Raymond Moriyama, architect of Toronto's City Hall and recently elected RIBA International Fellow, is clearly to be seen here, but Alexander Rankin was crucial to its refined realization.

The chaos and destruction of war has been choreographed into assured spaces and forms with raw materials, to create an iconic and successful building. Emerging from the landscape on one side, it faces the town on the other. The architectural spaces of remembrance and reconciliation, along with the rooftop walk – which collects you from one corner of the front of the building, sweeps you up and over the grassed roof and deposits you at the back – make the building very special.

The building takes a number of contemporary architectural tropes and fuses them in a remarkably coherent manner. The wondrous routes over and through the building set up a series of relationships, sometimes poignant, sometimes thrilling, between past and present, inside and outside, the brutal and the human.

This is a very large building (about 300 m long) and includes a huge amount of material at every scale. The dilemma was how to plan for large numbers of one-off visitors, while also creating a memorial for those who come more than once; how to respond to the city on one side and a more pastoral environment on the other; and how to create a civic facility for the city as a whole. The architectural solution works extremely well, starting with an impressive entrance lobby (large enough to seat six hundred for dinner) that can also act as a through route; the diagram of circulation and facilities is admirably clear, separating the main intense exhibition areas from other facilities and more intimate spaces, which include a memorial chapel, a regeneration hall and an artwork 'corridor'. Good but discreet access provision is another welcome feature of this museum.

CLIENT CANADIAN WAR MUSEUM
STRUCTURAL ENGINEER ADJELEIAN ALLEN RUBELI LTD
MECHANICAL ENGINEER THE MITCHELL PARTNERSHIP INC.
CONTRACTOR PCL CONSTRUCTORS CANADA INC.
CONTRACT VALUE CAN$96 MILLION
GROSS INTERNAL AREA 40,860 SQUARE METRES
PHOTOGRAPHERS HARRY FOSTER/TOM ARBAN

.THE LUBETKIN PRIZE

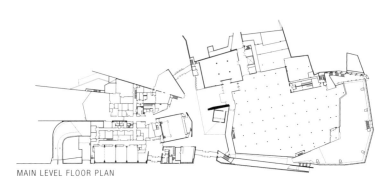

MAIN LEVEL FLOOR PLAN

50 .THE LUBETKIN PRIZE

51 .THE LUBETKIN PRIZE

TERRENCE DONNELLY CENTRE .TORONTO, CANADA .BEHNISCH ARCHITEKTEN WITH ARCHITECTS ALLIANCE

Laboratories are frequently dispiriting places, devoid of any architectural idea other than functional adjacencies. The Terrence Donnelly Centre for Biomolecular Research proves that this need not be so. It is a striking contribution to the university area of Toronto, and redefines its immediate architectural context, partly by contrast and partly by connection. It is a sophisticated and elegant urban response, which makes a virtue of its proximity to the existing university building. A nicely judged landscaped approach leads to a generous lobby and an entry sequence that would grace any headquarters building. A public ground-floor thoroughfare pays homage to Le Corbusier with light chutes and free-form mosaic-clad asymmetrical pods – an indication of the molecular science discussed within – which provide ground-floor meeting rooms. An atrium garden, filled with bamboo trees, rises six storeys, giving occupants a spectacular view as they emerge from their laboratories. Further up the building punched bays provide break-out space for the researchers, with views across the city. The laboratories themselves benefit from a relatively high degree of natural light, an absence of suspended ceilings and a clear plan form, with labs on the east side, a central service spine and a circulation corridor on the west side. The architecture as a whole is an exercise in combining strong forms with environmental thinking. Each elevation is treated separately, playing deftly with differing elevational treatments: the southern double-glazed façade provides a strong transparent face to the main street entrance, and appropriate solar and acoustic control. Fritting and coloured panels are used on the other façades in response to the activity behind (workspace or circulation space).

The new sciences demand new spaces, and this building dextrously provides them. Airy laboratories, a multitude of informal break-out spaces for those snatched conversations in which eighty per cent of breakthroughs are made, a connection back to nature and an entrance sequence to die for – together these summon up the dynamism of discovery.

This building says: science matters.

CLIENT UNIVERSITY OF TORONTO
STRUCTURAL ENGINEERS YOLLES PARTNERSHIP/KNIPPERS & HELBIG
MECHANICAL ENGINEER H.H. ANGUS & ASSOCIATES
LANDSCAPE DESIGN DIANNA GERRARD
CONTRACT VALUE € 46.4 MILLION
GROSS INTERNAL AREA 20,500 SQUARE METRES
PHOTOGRAPHERS TOM ARBAN/DAVID COOK

GROUND-FLOOR PLAN

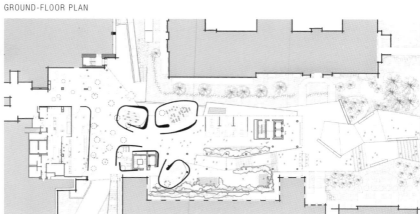

55 .THE LUBETKIN PRIZE

RIBA SPECIAL AWARDS

The RIBA special awards are chosen from RIBA Award-winners and are judged by panels that include specialist judges in the various fields, who pay further visits to the shortlisted buildings. These six awards reflect the diversity of architecture and reward the wide variety of specialist skills involved in delivering good buildings.

THE CROWN ESTATE CONSERVATION AWARD
SUPPORTED BY THE CROWN ESTATE

The Crown Estate Conservation Award is made to the architect of the best work of conservation that demonstrates successful restoration and/or adaptation of an architecturally significant building. It carries a prize of £5000. Previous winners have included Peter Inskip and Peter Jenkins for the Temple of Concord and Victory, Stowe; Foster and Partners for The Reichstag, Berlin, and the JC Decaux UK Headquarters, London; Rick Mather Architects for Dulwich Picture Gallery, London; Richard Murphy Architects with Simpson Brown Architects for the Stirling Tolbooth; LDN Architects for Newhailes House Conservation, Musselburgh; HOK International for the King's Library at the British Museum, London; and, last year, Avanti Architects for Isokon (Lawn Road) Apartments, London.

The Crown Estate manages a large and uniquely diverse portfolio of land and buildings across the UK. One of its primary concerns is to demonstrate that conservation is not a dry academic discipline, but the practical art of making yesterday's buildings work for people today.

The award was judged by Richard Griffiths, conservation architect; David Pickles, senior architect in the Conservation Department of English Heritage; Roger Bright, chief executive of The Crown Estate; and Tony Chapman, RIBA head of awards. They visited:
CHRIST CHURCH SPITALFIELDS, LONDON, BY PURCELL MILLER TRITTON IN ASSOCIATION WITH WILLIAM WHITFIELD AND PARTNERS; NATIONAL GALLERY, EAST WING AND CENTRAL PORTICO, PHASE I, LONDON, BY DIXON JONES WITH PURCELL MILLER TRITTON; PINIONS BARN, HIGHAM CROSS, BY SIMON CONDER ASSOCIATES; HARBOUR MEADOW, CHICHESTER, BY AVANTI ARCHITECTS; AND THE EGG, BATH, BY HAWORTH TOMPKINS.

The winner was the NATIONAL GALLERY, EAST WING AND CENTRAL PORTICO.

NATIONAL GALLERY, EAST WING + CENTRAL PORTICO .LONDON WC2 .DIXON JONES WITH PURCELL MILLER TRITTON

Creative conservation is not just about caring for the fabric of historic buildings; it is also about adapting them to accommodate new needs, with old and new co-existing to their mutual advantage. This complicated project, which both reveals the splendour of the historical main entrance sequence and provides for the needs of today's visitors, shows how this can be achieved in an exemplary manner.

With the continual growth of its collection as well as the changing requirements and expectations of visitors, the National Gallery has been engaged in an almost continual state of change since its inception in the early nineteenth century. This project represents further change as part of an ingenious and ambitious three-phase masterplan commissioned in 1998, designed to improve access and relieve pressure on the portico entrance, as well as providing visitor facilities appropriate to a building of national importance.

Phase 1 involved adapting the East Wing portico to provide, for the first time, a fully accessible street-level entrance from Trafalgar Square. This highly permeable glazed entrance provides enticing views into the gallery as well as splendid views from the gallery on to the now-pedestrianized square. A new shop and café are symmetrically placed to either side of the new entrance hall. From the foyer the route leads to the dramatic new Annenberg Court that occupies one of the eight historic internal courtyards and forms a generous top-lit space providing a link to various levels.

Phase 2 tackled the central portico entrance. Here some bold engineering to remove structure supporting the dome has transformed the entrance from a collection of cramped rooms into a series of clearly linked spaces. This understated intervention has provided a deeply satisfying fusion of the old with the new. Phase 2 has also recovered the J.D. Crace decoration to the Staircase Hall and Central Hall that formed part of the works undertaken by Sir John Taylor in 1887. Overpainting added in the 1960s has been removed and a scholarly and meticulous reinstatement of the polychromatic decoration

CLIENT NATIONAL GALLERY
STRUCTURAL ENGINEER ALAN BAXTER ASSOCIATES
SERVICES ENGINEER ANDREW REID & PARTNERS
QS GARDINER & THEOBALD
CONTRACTOR WATES CONSTRUCTION LTD
CONTRACT VALUE £14.5 MILLION
DATE OF COMPLETION SEPTEMBER 2005
GROSS INTERNAL AREA 3500 SQUARE METRES (RENOVATION)/1000 SQUARE METRES (NEW BUILD)
PHOTOGRAPHER NATIONAL GALLERY

ALSO SHORTLISTED FOR THE RIBA INCLUSIVE DESIGN AWARD
NATIONAL GALLERY SHORTLISTED FOR THE RIBA/ARTS COUNCIL ENGLAND CLIENT OF THE YEAR

has been carried out. An added benefit has been the introduction of discreet air conditioning, allowing the Central Hall to become a showcase for some of the most important paintings in the collection, enormously enriching the visitor route.

Managing change to a Grade I-listed building of national importance brings serious challenges if significance is not to be compromised or eroded. This project has revealed and reinforced the values that make this building so special, while greatly improving the visitors' experience.

The original RIBA Awards judges said: 'This project forms the first two of three phases deriving from a hundred-year health check on the gallery. The other main driver of the scheme was the acquisition of St Vincent House, to the north of the Sainsbury Wing, which could be used to decant staff from the Wilkins Building so that could be given over entirely to public space.

'The modifications to the entrance now provide direct access to and from Trafalgar Square; this has greatly enhanced the movement annually of five and a half million visitors through the gallery and its ancillary spaces. The new interiors are an understated, modernist fusion of the old with the new.

'The removal of large piers and the insertion of trusses to support the accommodation above were bold strokes and have enlarged the entrance foyer. This thoughtful and intelligent intervention has enhanced this important interior. Barrier-free disabled access directly from Trafalgar Square is possible for the first time.

'The work is very much in the spirit of the opening up of the neighbouring National Portrait Gallery through the reclamation of dead space. It is no co-incidence that the two projects involved the same client, Charles Saumarez Smith, whose inspired thinking is to be commended every bit as much as the architects' brilliant implementation.'

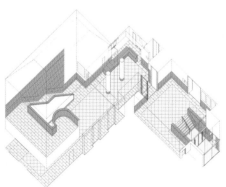

AXONOMETRIC OF EAST ENTRANCE

THE MANSER MEDAL
SPONSORED BY THE ARCHITECTS' JOURNAL

The Manser Medal is awarded for the best one-off house designed by an architect in the UK. The award is judged by a panel including Michael Manser CBE, past president of the RIBA; Robert Dye, architect and winner of the 2005 Manser Medal; Niall McLaughlin, architect, incoming chair of the RIBA Awards Group; and Tony Chapman, RIBA head of awards.

All the RIBA Award-winning houses and major extensions in the UK were considered for this year's Manser Medal, and five were shortlisted: HOLLY BARN, REEDHAM, NORFOLK, BY KNOX BHAVAN ARCHITECTS; ESHER HOUSE, ESHER, BY WILKINSON KING ARCHITECTS; BRICK HOUSE, LONDON W2, BY CARUSO ST JOHN ARCHITECTS; LIGHT HOUSE, LONDON W11, BY GIANNI BOTSFORD ARCHITECTS; AND WRAP HOUSE, LONDON W4, BY ALISON BROOKS ARCHITECTS.

The winner was HOLLY BARN.

HOLLY BARN
.REEDHAM, NORFOLK .KNOX BHAVAN ARCHITECTS

The judging was particularly difficult this year, with the debate polarizing between architecture that was able to achieve truly sublime spaces, and responses to context and brief that were so thorough and imaginative that they could stand as exemplars for housing everywhere. Holly Barn finally won because it is a mature and fully thought-through home for a wheelchair-bound client, for whom the design and realization have transformed his living experience to one of daily joy. Many homes designed for disabled people shout about their inclusive credentials. This one does not – the owner says that sometimes when he is working there, he completely forgets that he is disabled.

Built in the horizontal landscape of the Norfolk Broads, this new home stands alone, beyond the other village houses, on the site of a derelict agricultural shed. On the windswept day the Manser judges visited, the usual projections and angles of eaves and ridge of the two-storey barn seemed to have been scoured away by the elements. With timber boarding wrapping walls and roof, it sits effortlessly in a local vernacular tradition of windmills, boat-houses and boats under sail on the Broads one hundred metres away.

The main surprise lies inside, with the inversion of sleeping and living: on entering, a double-height space with a timber stair beside a purpose-made wheelchair lift leads up to a galleried kitchen. Far from perverse, this arrangement is exactly what the client demanded. Upstairs, the pitched roof is expressed as a continuous volume with partitions topped by glazing up to the hooped ceiling. The first-floor side walls are almost continuous timber-framed windows, but set slightly lower than usual to open up the landscape to a wheelchair user. Down the side of central service pods runs a wheelchair-width space with cleverly detailed sliding doors and open living areas at each end (one is the master bedroom). This is a beguiling example of single-space living with all the functional flexibility of cellular division, and a joyful response to a particular, unusual and demanding brief.

CLIENTS ALAN AND JENNY ROGERS
STRUCTURAL ENGINEER ECKERSLEY O'CALLAGHAN
LANDSCAPE ARCHITECT BUCKLEY DESIGN ASSOCIATES
CONTRACTOR WILLOW BUILDERS
CONTRACT VALUE £500,000
DATE OF COMPLETION DECEMBER 2005
GROSS INTERNAL AREA 260 SQUARE METRES
PHOTOGRAPHER DENNIS GILBERT – VIEW

ALSO SHORTLISTED FOR THE RIBA INCLUSIVE DESIGN AWARD

The house achieves a high standard of sustainability, not only in materials and construction, but also in using orientation to harness solar heat and light to the lower recreation and guest-bedroom floor while naturally minimizing heat loss and extending the thermal response of the structure. Upstairs, the large sliding window-wall elements afford maximum cross-ventilation in summer and passive heat gain in winter, with light bouncing deep into the plan from the curved ceiling vault.

The simplicity of form is misleading: this is a meticulously considered project in design and resolution of the brief, in construction and in detailing.

The RIBA Awards judges said: 'From outside, the long, low structure, with its Dutch-barn-like hooped roof, takes the breath away. The natural timber boarding on walls and roof chimes well with the local vernacular. It is so fresh in detail and in its use of materials, in complete contrast to the very ordinary bungalows and houses in the vicinity.

'Internally, the attractive and diverse spaces are set out in logical order with the more public rooms at the entrance end, leading to the more private rooms beyond. The ground floor contains the entrance hall, a games room and guest bedrooms. Unusually for a house designed largely around the needs of a disabled person, the main living rooms – dining kitchen, lounge and study – are on the first floor. And why not? That is what the client wanted and there are plenty of well-integrated and well-detailed special access features to make it all work. Large sliding screens open to allow the summer in and make the most of the views of the Broadland scenery. At the far end is the master bedroom with the best view of all.

'Throughout the interior are special access features for the wheelchair-bound owner. All are well integrated, including some ingenious details such as recesses for handles enabling doors to open flush against the wall. Holly Barn is a building perfectly in tune with its ambition to create a fully accessible house for all who use it.'

FIRST-FLOOR PLAN

69 .THE MANSER MEDAL

THE RIBA/ARTS COUNCIL ENGLAND CLIENT OF THE YEAR

The RIBA set up the Client of the Year award with Arts Council England nine years ago to honour the key role that a good client plays in the creation of fine architecture. Good architecture needs clients with both faith and vision. Everyone has benefited from the taste and persistence of good clients, from the Medicis to the city of Manchester.

Architecture is a team effort, as previous winners have amply demonstrated: Roland Paoletti, who received the first award for the new Jubilee Line stations; the MCC for a series of fine buildings at Lord's Cricket Ground; the Foreign and Commonwealth Office for a series of iconic embassies around the world; the Moledinar Park Housing Association in Glasgow for its campus of buildings by Scottish architects; Urban Splash for its commitment both to design quality and to the regeneration of Manchester and Liverpool; the City of Manchester for transforming its public realm with a range of post-IRA-bomb projects; the Peabody Trust for pioneering work in off-site construction, the realization of truly sustainable housing and, in particular, its RIBA-Award-winning schemes at Raines Court, London, by Allford Hall Monaghan Morris, at Murray Grove by Cartwright Pickard, and BedZED by Bill Dunster Architects; and, last year, Gateshead Council for commissioning a series of major projects, each of which has contributed to the regeneration of the town and each of which resulted from well-run competitions: Sage, the Millennium Bridge, Baltic: Centre for Contemporary Art, and the Angel of the North.

Judging was by members of the RIBA's Awards Group, chaired by architects Jeremy Till and Claire Booth representing Arts Council England. They considered clients of RIBA Award-winning schemes of the past two years but took into account a track record of successful commissioning, particularly where this has led to RIBA Awards.

DAVIES ALPINE HOUSE, KEW (NICK GUTTRIDGE)
SACKLER CROSSING, KEW (ROYAL BOTANIC GARDENS)

The 2006 shortlist was:
MAGGIE'S CENTRES, for its expanding network of cancer-care centres, including the award-winner by Page\Park in Inverness; the ROYAL BOTANIC GARDENS, for commissioning a series of fine buildings, including the award-winning Davies

Alpine House at Kew by Wilkinson Eyre; QUEEN MARY UNIVERSITY, LONDON, for using good architects to enrich a disparate campus of buildings, in particular for the award-winning Institute of Cell and Molecular Science by SMC Alsop/Amec Design & Management, and the Lock-keeper's Graduate Centre by Surface Architects; and the NATIONAL GALLERY, LONDON, and its director, Charles Saumarez Smith, working with Dixon Jones to transform the public face of the gallery, making it fully accessible, and commissioning Dixon Jones and Purcell Miller Tritton to conserve some of the fine Wilkins interiors.

The winner was the ROYAL BOTANIC GARDENS.

The Royal Botanic Gardens has commissioned a series of fine buildings at Kew and its country cousin, Wakehurst Place. At Kew, Wilkinson Eyre has produced a masterplan into which it has inserted the award-winning Davies Alpine House. The granite and bronze Sackler Crossing by John Pawson adopts 'Capability' Brown's 'sinuous Line of Grace' as it hugs the water, so pedestrians feel they are walking on the surface of the lake.

At Wakehurst Place, a 500-acre estate in West Sussex, Walters and Cohen designed the 2005 RIBA Award-winning visitor centre, a restrained and sensitively located glass, steel and timber building that sits very comfortably within the landscape. It acts as a foil to Stanton Williams's 2001 RIBA Award-winning scheme, the Millennium Seedbank, a low barrel-vaulted building inspired by the surrounding landscape, designed to maximize energy conservation while providing the best possible conditions for seed storage.

The Royal Botanic Gardens' ever-growing portfolio of good architecture complements unique landscapes and the architectural and engineering heritage of the Victorian greenhouses. It also facilitates vital scientific work and enhances the experience of millions of visitors to the two gardens. For an ongoing commitment to the commissioning of excellent architecture, the Royal Botanic Gardens was named the RIBA/Arts Council England Client of the Year for 2006.

VISITOR CENTRE, WAKEHURST PLACE (COURTESY DAISY HUTCHISON/WALTERS AND COHEN)
MILLENNIUM SEEDBANK, WAKEHURST PLACE (PETER COOK – VIEW)

THE RIBA INCLUSIVE DESIGN AWARD
IN ASSOCIATION WITH THE CENTRE FOR ACCESSIBLE ENVIRONMENTS AND NICHOLLS & CLARKE

This award celebrates inclusivity in building design and encapsulates an important new design philosophy. The principles of inclusive design are articulated as follows: it places people at the heart of the design process; acknowledges human diversity and difference; offers choice where a single design solution cannot accommodate all users; provides for flexibility in use; and aims to provide buildings that are safe, convenient, equitable and enjoyable to use by everyone, regardless of ability, age or gender.

The previous winners of the RIBA Inclusive Design Award were City of Manchester Stadium, by Arup Associates, and Sage Gateshead, by Foster and Partners. Winners of the predecessor prize, The ADAPT Trust Access Award, were the Royal Academy of Dramatic Arts (RADA), London, by Avery Associates; Dance Base, Edinburgh, by Malcolm Fraser Architects; and The Space, Dundee College, by Nicholl Russell Studios.

This year's award was judged by Sarah Langton-Lockton, chief executive of the Centre for Accessible Environments; David Spooner, director of research and development at Nicholls & Clarke, the leading designer, manufacturer and supplier of access products; and Tony Chapman, the RIBA's head of awards. They visited:
HOLLY BARN, REEDHAM, NORFOLK, BY KNOX BHAVAN ARCHITECTS; THE EGG, BATH, BY HAWORTH TOMPKINS; EVELINA CHILDREN'S HOSPITAL, LONDON SE1, BY HOPKINS ARCHITECTS; IDEA STORE WHITECHAPEL, LONDON E1, BY ADJAYE/ASSOCIATES; AND THE NATIONAL GALLERY EAST WING AND CENTRAL PORTICO, LONDON WC2, BY DIXON JONES WITH PURCELL MILLER TRITTON.

The winner was IDEA STORE WHITECHAPEL.

The Idea Store is a truly inclusive building. The judges particularly admired the way in which it encapsulates so many of the principles of inclusive design and puts them into action. It is not just a statement; it is a living, breathing and inclusive place.

The Idea Store concept is being refined in each of its successive manifestations. At Whitechapel both client and architect have learnt from the experience of the Chrisp Street store, also in Tower Hamlets, east London, and created a building that really does speak to its community. This is demonstrated by recent research showing that the user profile of the building exactly matches the ethnic make-up of the borough.

It also shows the importance of a vision shared by an enlightened client and a responsive architect. Together they have conceived, planned and created a building that functions brilliantly not only as a library but also as a much broader resource for the community – open twelve hours a day on weekdays and at weekends – giving citizens meeting spaces and seminar rooms, a dance studio and therapy room, and a café-cum-reading room.

The Idea Store represents a successful contemporary reinvention of a building type. As a library it is inviting, not inhibiting, welcoming rather than off-putting. It adopts many of the facets of a building type that is more familiar to everyone: the shop. On entering, instead of the barrier of an issue desk the user sees shelves of DVDs. There are computer terminals everywhere and in configurations to suit all, from open-plan to one-off workstations in quiet corners. Yet far from debasing the idea of the library, the Idea Store broadens and deepens it. Signage is a part of the story: it is both funky and user-friendly, genuinely adding to the usability of the building.

This is no set-piece, imposed on the local community. It is a fun place to be, with a buzz you can feel the moment you walk through the door or mount the escalator. And it has street cred: whoever thought anyone would say that of a library?

FOR BUILDING CITATION, SEE PAGES 28–29.

THE RIBA SUSTAINABILITY AWARD
SPONSORED BY ENGLISH PARTNERSHIPS

This award is made to the building that demonstrates most elegantly and durably the principles of sustainable architecture. The prize was established in 2000, when the winner was Chetwood Associates' Sainsbury's at Greenwich. The other winners have been Michael Hopkins and Partners' Jubilee Campus, University of Nottingham; the Cardboard School, Westborough Primary School, Westcliff-on-Sea, by Cottrell + Vermeulen Architecture; BedZED, Wallington, by Bill Dunster Architects; Stock Orchard Street, London N7, by Sarah Wigglesworth Architects; and, last year, Cobtun House, Worcester, by Associated Architects.

The award was judged by a panel of experts comprising Jeremy Till, chair of the RIBA Awards Group; Nick Thompson, architect and a member of the RIBA's Sustainable Futures Committee; and John Callcutt, chief executive of English Partnerships. They visited:
ARC, HULL, BY NIALL MCLAUGHLIN ARCHITECTS; NATIONAL ASSEMBLY FOR WALES, CARDIFF, BY RICHARD ROGERS PARTNERSHIP; HEELIS, SWINDON, BY FEILDEN CLEGG BRADLEY ARCHITECTS; AND UCL SCHOOL OF SLAVONIC AND EAST EUROPEAN STUDIES, LONDON WC1, BY SHORT AND ASSOCIATES.

The winner was HEELIS.

HEELIS
.SWINDON .FEILDEN CLEGG BRADLEY ARCHITECTS

In many ways this is the most straightforward of the four schemes shortlisted for the RIBA Sustainability Award, but it is also the project with the most transferable lessons. It is primarily a basic building type: a developer-built office block (The National Trust leases the building). That it can raise the sustainable stakes as high as it does is the real achievement. Built by a developer at standard Class A costs, additional expense for the sustainable elements was allowed only where it fitted into a ten-year payback.

The sustainable design is quite simple but well delivered: a well-handled natural-ventilation system with a degree of user control, super-insulation, photovoltaics, lots of daylight, and sensor-controlled lighting. There is something very direct about the strategy that makes it understandable both to the occupants and to the public, so important lessons can be passed on. The building was described to the judges as a 'cardigan building': you learn to adapt to its cycles by putting on and taking off layers – something that was seen as positive by both client and judges.

However, most importantly, the strategy delivers an exceptionally pleasant working environment that feels healthy without being excessively worthy. Use of daylight, disposition of courtyards and atria, and placing of windows are all brilliantly judged to give a sense of the outside and openness, while at the same time occupants are not left feeling exposed. For such a big building it is also surprisingly intimate, and the disarmingly simple construction never descends to crudeness.

The National Trust has furthered the sustainable ethos of the design through its management practices with some simple ideas (no individual bins under desks, just central recycling points) and some that are more demanding (no car-parking spaces unless you are part of a car-share).

The judges of this special award were pleased to be able to give the prize to a

CLIENTS THE NATIONAL TRUST/KIER PROPERTIES
ENVIRONMENTAL ENGINEER MAX FORDHAM PARTNERSHIP
STRUCTURAL ENGINEER ADAMS KARA TAYLOR
LANDSCAPE ARCHITECT GRANT ASSOCIATES
QS DAVIS LANGDON
PROJECT MANAGER BURO FOUR
CONTRACTOR MOSS CONSTRUCTION
CONTRACT VALUE £14.5 MILLION
DATE OF COMPLETION JUNE 2005
GROSS INTERNAL AREA 7260 SQUARE METRES
PHOTOGRAPHER SIMON DOLING

'mainstream' building type, sending out the signal that sustainability can and should be claimed by the centre ground, and not be seen as the exclusive domain of the one-off or maverick experiment.

The RIBA Awards judges were equally enthusiastic: 'Won in a design competition, this striking building is the very antithesis of what one might expect The National Trust to provide for itself. The generous front-of-house provides a welcoming reception, a shop and a café that is open to the public. The building was procured as a commercial turn-key operation and the client team was crucial to the whole operation, with an architect facilities manager working closely with the design team throughout. He then collaborated with the environmental engineers for the whole of the first year of operation to tune the ambitious engineering.

'The triangular shape is a response to the surrounding geometries and offers an elegant thin-columned colonnade as part of a striking south elevation that incorporates robust grilles through which the cooling night air enters. The whole two-storey deep-plan office is daylit and naturally ventilated with a myriad of chimneys. The performance of the banks of photovoltaics on the roof is displayed in the entrance hall. The quality of air and light inside, the two accessible internal courtyard gardens, the state-of-the-art office layout and the great atrial sitting room and staff canteen have gone a long way to satisfy an initially sceptical staff: sceptical about moving to Swindon, about the use of their cars being restricted to car-sharers, and about open-plan offices for all, up to and including the director-general.

'This beautifully restrained project has more than fulfilled the client's expectations. Four hundred building users are now enthusiastic about this model low-energy office building on a brownfield site. Ongoing monitoring will provide useful knowledge for architects and engineers involved on similar projects. The detailing is of a very high standard, the delightful furnishings specified by the client work well with the architecture, and the exterior brickwork is a tour de force.'

GROUND-FLOOR PLAN

78 .THE RIBA SUSTAINABILITY AWARD

THE STEPHEN LAWRENCE PRIZE
IN ASSOCIATION WITH THE MARCO GOLDSCHMIED FOUNDATION

The Stephen Lawrence Prize is sponsored by the Marco Goldschmied
Foundation. It commemorates the teenager who was just setting out on the
road to becoming an architect when he was murdered in 1993. It rewards
the best examples of projects with a construction budget of less than
£1 million. In addition to the £5000 prize money, Marco Goldschmied
provides £10,000 to fund the Stephen Lawrence Scholarship at the
Architectural Association in London.

The prize was set up in 1998 to draw attention to the Stephen Lawrence
Trust, which assists young black students to study architecture, and to reward
smaller projects and the creativity required when architects are working with
low budgets. Previous winners have been Ian Ritchie Architects, for the
Terrasson Cultural Greenhouse, France; Munkenbeck + Marshall, for the
Sculpture Gallery at Roche Court, near Salisbury; Softroom Architects, for the
Kielder Belvedere in Northumberland; Richard Rose-Casemore, for the
Hatherley Studio, Winchester; Cottrell + Vermeulen, for the Cardboard
Building at Westborough Primary School, Westcliff-on-Sea; Gumuchdjian
Architects, for Think Tank, Skibbereen; Simon Conder Associates, for Vista,
Dungeness; and Niall McLaughlin Architects, for the House at Clonakilty,
County Cork.

The 2006 award was judged by architect Marco Goldschmied,
Doreen Lawrence OBE, journalist David Taylor and architect David Adjaye.
They visited:
BROUGHTON HALL PAVILION, SKIPTON, BY HOPKINS ARCHITECTS; PINIONS BARN, HIGHAM
CROSS, BUCKINGHAMSHIRE, BY SIMON CONDER ASSOCIATES; THE DAVIES ALPINE HOUSE, ROYAL
BOTANIC GARDENS, KEW, BY WILKINSON EYRE; LOCK–KEEPER'S GRADUATE CENTRE, LONDON E1,
BY SURFACE ARCHITECTS; AND WRAP HOUSE, LONDON W4, BY ALISON BROOKS ARCHITECTS.

The winner was WRAP HOUSE.

WRAP HOUSE
.LONDON W4 .ALISON BROOKS ARCHITECTS

This house extension in Chiswick, west London, is an exemplary adaptation: the judges were immediately taken with its passion and joy. Its subtle geometry creates a series of high-quality spaces, using well-chosen materials, that is a tribute to the design team's skill and flair. The intelligent, effortless connection to the Edwardian house has transformed it, adding value while satisfying a client on a tight budget. In the lottery that is the UK planning system, the scheme was undoubtedly helped by its luck in having a planning officer who clearly understood the value of good design.

The Wrap House embraces its outside spaces elegantly and effectively, integrating an old tree with the wooden decking and treating the roof as a dynamic and beautiful elevation in its own right. The judges admired the way this origami-like roof appears to fold and – through its triangulated geometry – allows views of the back garden from the house's master bedroom. The project is also a tribute to the Canadian clients, who ignored the contractor-led procurement route all too common for UK 'back extensions' – a commendable approach and one to be fully supported and endorsed.

The RIBA Awards judges said: 'A humble commission for a domestic rear extension has become a thing of wonder and delight. The project comprises an addition to a house in which the simple idea of a dining-room extension has been broadened to create a complex series of spaces that colonizes the garden with sliding glazed doors opening out on to a terrace.

'The savvy client was well aware that views of the extension – from an upstairs window or from the garden – are as important as views out from it. By taking the 65-square-metre space right across the rear elevation, the architect has given the illusion of a much bigger volume than the planners stipulated (doubtless they have checked and checked). Subtle inflections of the roof mirror the pitch of the roofs of the Edwardian house and its neighbours and lend it a sense of weightlessness. The sliding glazed doors open on the corner, emphasizing the inside/outside experience. The impression of dematerialization is furthered by framing the glazing with

CLIENTS MARK AND ADRIANNE BREWER
STRUCTURAL ENGINEER PRICE & MYERS
CONTRACTOR STIDWORTHY BUILDING
CONTRACT VALUE £161,000
DATE OF COMPLETION OCTOBER 2005
GROSS INTERNAL AREA 65 SQUARE METRES
PHOTOGRAPHER CRISTOBAL PALMA

ALSO SHORTLISTED FOR THE MANSER MEDAL

vertical polished-steel columns, which the eye slides round, and by the use of mirrors. It all sounds rather tricksy, but it is not; it is clever, making much of really very little.

'The extension is separated from the Edwardian house by a glazed link, giving the impression that it is a pavilion in its own right. The timber deck, walls and roof are carefully detailed and emphasize the clarity of the architect's vision encapsulated in the name, Wrap House.

'The Wrap House shows how the humble house extension can form a fertile testing ground for experimental architecture. The architects made extensive use of computer-3D and physical modelling until they were satisfied that the design resolved all the issues concerning structure, planning, internal spatial conditions, existing views and drainage. They also borrowed technologies from other forms of construction, including obviating the need for disruptive foundations by using an elevated concrete slab supported on miniature concrete piles – a system more common in commercial buildings. The result shows what can be achieved when architect, client and contractor share ambition, dedication and a willingness to communicate.

'Confidence is apparent in the formulation of the design parameters, in the quality of the detailing and in the implementation. The design is exquisite and inspiring, creating complexity out of a simple proposition, something ethereal and outstanding. The modest brief and small budget further emphasize the skill of the architect in delivering a beautiful little building.'

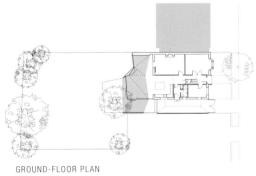

GROUND-FLOOR PLAN

85 .THE STEPHEN LAWRENCE PRIZE

THE RIBA AWARDS

Established in 1966, the RIBA Awards comprised both national and regional awards until the creation of the Stirling Prize in 1996. Since then all the awards have been national, but they are still judged by regional juries. They are first considered by a regional panel (and visited if there is any doubt as to whether they should progress further); a shortlist is then visited by the regional jury, including an architect from the region, one from elsewhere and a 'lay' juror – an engineer, client, artist or journalist, etc. The chairs of the fourteen regional juries make their cases to the Awards Group (the scheme's advisory panel), which has the right to challenge recommendations and to query buildings visited but not recommended. If there is no agreement, members of the Awards Group have to pay what might be a third visit. True to the principle that no project is rejected by people who have not seen it, they have the final say. Confirmed awards are announced and celebrated at a dinner in June. Shortlists for the Stirling Prize and all the other special awards are selected from these winners and winners of the RIBA European Awards.

RIBA European Awards and RIBA International Awards are awards in their own right and are judged by members of the RIBA Awards Group. Shortlisting is done from careful consideration of entry material including an A1 panel, and shortlisted schemes are then visited.

Assessors are listed in the order: chair, regional representative, lay assessor
SCOTLAND Robert Adam, Riccardo Marini, Dennis Gilbert
NORTHERN IRELAND Gordon Murray, Alan Jones, Hank Dittmar
NORTH-WEST Paul Hyett, David McCall, Simon Calder
NORTH-EAST Tony Kettle, Carl Meddings, Jane Wernick
WALES Dominic Williams, Jonathan Adams, Steven Rose
WEST MIDLANDS Keith Williams, Chris Cronin/Alan McBeth, Mike Hayes
EAST MIDLANDS Jonathan Ellis Miller, Kanti Chhapi, Kester Rattenbury
EAST Will Alsop, Peter Goodwin, Bryan Appleyard
SOUTH-WEST Robin Nicholson, Michael Wigginton, Jane Mann
WESSEX Robin Nicholson, Jonathan Platt, Jane Mann
SOUTH David Adjaye, Andrew Salter, Edwin Heathcote
SOUTH-EAST David Marks, Sean Albuquerque, Robert Smith
LONDON EAST Alan Johnson/Andrew Hanson, Annalie Riches, Marcus Fairs
LONDON NORTH John Miller, Phyllida Mills, John Smith
LONDON SOUTH Graham Morrison, Henning Stummel, Colin Henderson
LONDON WEST John Assael, Terry Pawson, David Rosen
EUROPEAN AND INTERNATIONAL Cany Ash, Emily Campbell, Tony Chapman, Paul Finch, Richard Griffiths, Rachel Haugh, Glenn Howells, Edward Jones, Niall McLaughlin, Paul Monaghan, Sheila O'Donnell, Jeremy Till

JKS WORKSHOPS
.CLYDEBANK .GORDON MURRAY + ALAN DUNLOP
ARCHITECTS

The brief called for innovation in the design for a series of start-up industrial units. Inexpensive but with 'flair and architectural edge', they were to be part of a well-considered, firmly design-led catalyst to the regeneration of a rundown part of Glasgow. The response came in the form of L-shaped modules that define a service yard for deliveries and parking. The basic structures use standard materials, but enough budget was saved to wrap them in eye-catching skins: coloured fibre cement or anodized aluminium panels, which have bronzed nicely. At high level the 'Jenga' forms are clad in translucent polycarbonate, allowing soft daylight to filter into the units even on dull days.

There can be no more basic building than the windowless top-lit industrial shed. But put a series of such light-industrial units together, consider the whole as a large cubic composition, create a locally significant decoration (based on local employer Singer Sewing Machines's castle-stitch pattern) for some of the uniformly rectangular cladding panels, and add a talented designer, and this most unpromising type can become good architecture. With so few elements available, every detail counts. The combined industrial and access doors, the expressed asymmetrical frame, and the changes of plane between the high-level glazing and cladding all add elegance to the project.

This is a pioneering design in many senses and gives distinction to the most practical of functions. Security and access issues mean the complex turns its back on its urban surroundings, but it is rescued by the colour and pattern that add liveliness to the blank exteriors.

CLIENT CLYDEBANK REBUILT LTD
STRUCTURAL ENGINEER WOOLGAR HUNTER
SERVICES ENGINEER HENDERSON WARNOCK
QS GARDINER AND THEOBALD
CONTRACTOR LUDDON CONSTRUCTION LTD
CONTRACT VALUE £1.7 MILLION
DATE OF COMPLETION OCTOBER 2005
GROSS INTERNAL AREA 1700 SQUARE METRES
PHOTOGRAPHER ANTHONY COLEMAN

MAGGIE'S HIGHLANDS CANCER CARING CENTRE, RAIGMORE HOSPITAL
.INVERNESS .PAGE\PARK ARCHITECTS

Since their early days Maggie's Centres have become synonymous with architectural virtuosity – although the innovation is all to a purpose. The Highlands Cancer Caring Centre rises to the delicate challenge with a consistent and powerful concept of a flattened ascending copper spiral. The stepped board-like copper cladding and the points of the broken spiral give the impression of a beached boat and a deceptively small scale.

In fact, the unifying metaphor for the scheme is cell-division, and these forms are reflected not only in the building, but also in the landscaping designed by Charles Jencks. Two vesica-shaped spiral mounds in the landscape combine with the building in a trilogy of dividing cells. The building can be seen (although admittedly best from the air) as an inversion of one of the mounds, walls angling out rather than in, with the copper bands echoing the paths that wind round the mounds.

The plain birch-ply interior opens up to a surprisingly large complex of volumes ascending into the spiral and creating a series of discrete but linked spaces that serve the required combination of privacy and community well. Exposed edge-grain birch-ply furniture and fittings, including the staircase, library shelves, kitchen worktops and bench seating, add to the pleasing continuity of the scheme.

This little building is remarkably good value for money thanks largely to the low-cost, low-tech timber frame (the only steel in the entire structure is in the screws, nails, straps, ties and plates that hold it all together). Combined with the matching drama of the garden, this is an extraordinary miniature monument that contrasts with the prosaic background of a conventional hospital complex.

CLIENT MAGGIE'S CENTRES
STRUCTURAL ENGINEER SKM ANTHONY HUNTS
SERVICES ENGINEER HARLEY HADDOW
LANDSCAPE DESIGNER CHARLES JENCKS
LANDSCAPE ARCHITECT GROSS MAX
QS THOMAS & ADAMSON
CONTRACTOR MORRISON CONSTRUCTION
CONTRACT VALUE £860,000
DATE OF COMPLETION MARCH 2005
GROSS INTERNAL AREA 225 SQUARE METRES
PHOTOGRAPHER KEITH HUNTER

MAGGIE'S CENTRES SHORTLISTED FOR THE RIBA/ARTS COUNCIL ENGLAND CLIENT OF THE YEAR

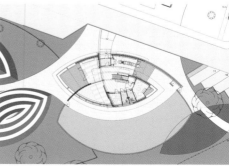

GROUND-FLOOR PLAN

THE SALTIRE CENTRE, GLASGOW CALEDONIAN UNIVERSITY
.GLASGOW .BUILDING DESIGN PARTNERSHIP

This complex and busy building is packed full of ideas, chief among them responses to the question: how can we improve the way we make libraries? Calling them learning centres is only a tiny start; it takes big thinking from architects and clients to engender significant change. Here the client was more than specific. He wanted to make it the primary university building, a place where people would want to be: inclusive, inviting, sociable, accessible and encouraging learning; modern, internally flexible, capable of future growth and change of use. A brief from heaven or hell, depending on the creativity of the architects reading it.

The new building acts a focus for student activity and adds drama and spatial excitement at a crossroads between existing buildings. Creating a powerful abstract image for the centre, a high sloping fritted-glass wall sheltering criss-crossing access bridges intersects with a pierced metal drum cladding a wide circular stair and lift. The wall also acts as a screen for lighting displays at night. This dramatic through-route divides the space into two: an open atrium outside and conventional floors inside. Simple variation of colour and opacity in a wall of cast lighting troughs makes a blind wall into a thing of interest.

This building is a dynamic spatial experience, contained by poor-quality existing buildings. None of this would have been possible without a supportive planning regime that encouraged a building that reached for the skies and made a flamboyant display of itself as it did so.

CLIENT GLASGOW CALEDONIAN UNIVERSITY
STRUCTURAL ENGINEER STRUER CONSULTING ENGINEERS
SERVICES CONSULTANT HULLEY & KIRKWOOD
LANDSCAPE DESIGN IAN WHITE ASSOCIATES
COST CONSULTANT CBA
CONTRACTOR BALFOUR BEATTY CONSTRUCTION
CONTRACT VALUE £15.5 MILLION
DATE OF COMPLETION JANUARY 2006
GROSS INTERNAL AREA 10,500 SQUARE METRES
PHOTOGRAPHERS DAVID BARBOUR/LES WATSON (TOP RIGHT)

GROUND-FLOOR PLAN

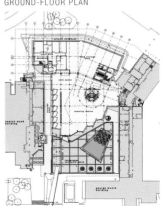

THE ARCHES CENTRE – HEALTH + CARE FOR EAST BELFAST .BELFAST .PENOYRE & PRASAD WITH TODD ARCHITECTS

This is a highly significant building in a number of ways: in terms of regeneration, procurement, healthcare design, and good design as a positive contribution to the healing process. It is one of the first manifestations of a pioneering procurement process developed by John Cole and the Department of Health in Northern Ireland: PRP (Performance Related Partnering), a design-based qualitative response to the vagaries of lowest-cost PFI. It is also a prototype for a new form of community-health building delivering decentralized hospital facilities at community level (there are already three in Belfast). It is exemplary on all counts. Over the last twenty years such accomplished and architecturally exciting public healthcare buildings have been rare in the UK.

The development creates what is effectively a healthcare shopping mall. Externally, the whole building acts as a marker for the community, making the most of a small budget. The use of coloured panels in the fenestration and an effective lighting system that connects with the artworks are the high spots: these link the two simple rendered prisms. Any sense of the meanness that usually obtains in staff areas has been avoided; here staff have been given the best roof-level views out across Belfast.

Internally, the street is reminiscent of Niels Torp's magnificent SAS HQ in Stockholm. The waiting-area pods break out from the rectilinearity of the main space to create interest, adding an intimate quality to the four-storey atrium and helping with orientation.

CLIENT SOUTH AND EAST BELFAST (HEALTH & SOCIAL SERVICES) TRUST
HEALTH-PLANNING ADVICE ANN NOBLE ARCHITECTS
STRUCTURAL ENGINEER PRICE & MYERS
SERVICES CONSULTANT MAX FORDHAM LLP
LANDSCAPE DESIGN GILLESPIES LLP
QS WHITE YOUNG GREEN
CONTRACTOR FARRANS CONSTRUCTION LTD
CONTRACT VALUE £8.6 MILLION
DATES OF COMPLETION AUGUST 2004 (PHASE 1)/SEPTEMBER 2005 (PHASE 2)
GROSS INTERNAL AREA 6300 SQUARE METRES
PHOTOGRAPHERS DENNIS GILBERT – VIEW/ PAUL MEGAHEY (BOTTOM)

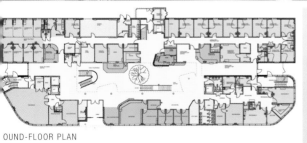

OUND-FLOOR PLAN

TRIPLICATE – OFFICE FIT-OUT
.BELFAST .HACKETT + HALL

A tight budget has been the inspiration for this wonderful project. The existing loft space – a new-build addition to a spec office conversion – has been left as an untouched envelope, with a series of objects inserted to delineate spaces. The placing of these objects changes the character and quality of the original open-plan space. The most significant is, in effect, a small building that could easily be imagined as a house or pavilion in an open landscape. This object-building contains offices and meeting spaces, and it is vested with such subtle moves and detailing that you long for a budget that would have allowed it to have been crafted in hardwood as a giant piece of furniture.

The major meeting space is shaped as a miniature auditorium, dividing the work and public meeting areas. In several places, including the rear wall, 'curtains' move across to modulate the public spaces, making them more intimate, secluded and private, as required. Flexibility is a driver here.

An enthusiastic client – a group of designers who have collaborated with the architects on subsequent projects – claims the new building has had a positive impact on business and on the well-being and enthusiasm of staff, in a workspace that sells their own capabilities to future clients.

CLIENT TRIPLICATE
STRUCTURAL ENGINEER ENNIS GRUHN & CO.
QS BAILIE CONNOR
CONTRACTOR PATTON FIT-OUT
CONTRACT VALUE £110,000
DATE OF COMPLETION MARCH 2005
GROSS INTERNAL AREA 380 SQUARE METRES
PHOTOGRAPHER GARY PARROT

LYMM WATER TOWER
.LYMM .ELLIS WILLIAMS ARCHITECTS

This is a project in which ambition, patience and determination have triumphed over adversity. After long battles with the planning authorities and neighbours, and with telecom companies who had rights to retain equipment on the tower, the result is a sophisticated and highly distinctive conversion and extension of a Grade II-listed structure. It has put back to use a building whose only remaining purpose had been as a plinth for mobile-phone antennae. And, in a witty but practical reference to its original use, a hot tub has been placed on the roof where client and guests can bathe under the light of the moon and Vodafone's now-shielded gaze.

The design is both sensitive and bold, refined in detail and robust in character. It is witty and playful in execution but serious in purpose. Minimalism is the overriding theme of the interiors, yet these are also practical and homely. A sensible compromise means that, rather than spreading accommodation over five floors, each with a limited foot-print, much of the living space is in the new build that wraps itself in a series of leaves, the geometry of which reflects the octagonal form of the tower.

Externally, the new is handled confidently, not just in the building extension, where roofs seemingly float above façades, but also in the soft and hard landscaping arrangements, where water features mysteriously penetrate under terraces and parts of the tower. The landscaping is consistently ordered within geometries that take their cue from the tower and its extensions, and this control continues to the very edge of the site.

Light, water and materials are managed to great effect to produce an accomplished and confident piece of work. So much is possible when designer and client work closely and confidently together – especially when they enjoy themselves, as they so evidently did here.

CLIENT THE HARRIS FAMILY
STRUCTURAL ENGINEER SINCLAIR KNIGHT MERZ
SERVICES CONSULTANT MILLER CONSULTING LTD
CONTRACTOR REDROW PLC
CONTRACT VALUE £500,000
DATE OF COMPLETION AUGUST 2004
GROSS INTERNAL AREA 500 SQUARE METRES
PHOTOGRAPHER JEREMY PHILIPS

GROUND-FLOOR PLAN

MOHO
.CASTLEFIELD, MANCHESTER .SHED KM

After World War II many cities and towns throughout the UK saw a new form of housing. Metal-windowed, factory-manufactured prefabs laid out in clusters, culs-de-sac or, more usually, streets with small gardens, these developments with their functional internal bathrooms and kitchens offered good space standards. With their modern appearance, these constructions gave us a glimpse of the potential of factory-built housing: despite their origins as temporary structures, there are prefabs still standing and they are much sought after.

Some sixty years later, as British housebuilders continue to produce dull and inefficient work, the efforts of Latham and, especially, Egan have inspired further attempts to develop a sophisticated form of factory-produced housing. Working on a tight site in a rundown district of Manchester, the developer Urban Splash has entered the fray with a seven-storey scheme comprising 102 apartments arranged in a U above two decks for car parking.

A series of unit variants and a clip-on conservatory option have the strict discipline and intelligence of an Ikea flat-pack. Take it or leave it, this is the deal: robust steel staircases and generously wide decks; big, almost industrial-scale, doors into living units; ingenious partitioning arrangements to maximize internal space flexibility; unusual arrangements such as baths entered from the end and not the side; and crisp, clean, if minimal, finishing. And on the street, freshness and warmth are offered by the timber shutter arrangements. Finally, add a well-landscaped inner courtyard that makes you think of warmer climes.

All this is great fun but underlying it is a very serious message: MoHo shows that there really is a role for factory-formed accommodation for dense urban living. Urban Splash and Shed KM offer the adventurous – young or old – a wonderful, robust and economical alternative.

CLIENT URBAN SPLASH
STRUCTURAL ENGINEER JOULE
SERVICES ENGINEER FULCRUM CONSULTING ENGINEERS
QS SIMON FENTON PARTNERSHIP
CONTRACTORS URBAN SPLASH BUILD/ YORKON
CONTRACT VALUE £8.9 MILLION
DATE OF OCCUPATION AUGUST 2005
PHOTOGRAPHER SHAW + SHAW

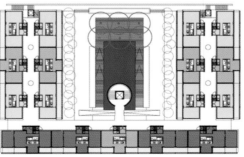

TYPICAL FLOOR PLAN

101 .NORTH-WEST

RESEARCH AREA FACILITY
.ALDERLEY PARK, MACCLESFIELD .AMEC DESIGN &
PROJECT SERVICES

A major drug company required state-of-the-art research laboratories in the form of a substantial 20,000-square-metre extension: this – the latest implementation of a masterplan by the Swedish architect Gert Wingardh – was inevitably a highly complex and demanding brief. Local planning constraints included a prohibition on anything that had an impact on the parkland setting and its rural prospect.

The result – on a site previously occupied by a car park – is a clear, functional and intelligent diagram, the simplicity of which eloquently masks the enormous sophistication of its planning. The new has been grafted on to the existing buildings, using them as internal façades on the sides of the street.

The careful design has produced a series of considered spaces, with an understated palette of colour and materials used throughout to unify the scheme. Light maple, applied everywhere, gives a gentle ambience; in the grand central street that runs the length of the building the same stone has been used on the floor as on the façades; and the strictly ordered laboratories are also clad externally in stone. Here the high standard of the detailing can be seen in the visible structure, construction and finishes, and the integration of building services. The ambience is closer to that of a studio than a laboratory.

This is a very large bespoke commercial project by a major design-and-build company using, in part, high-quality consultant architects for elements within the design. The successful collaboration of everyone involved demonstrates the real quality in design terms that can be achieved when an estates department demonstrates a worthy degree of ambition, safeguards it during procurement and pursues it to an intelligent conclusion.

CLIENT ASTRAZENECA
INTERIOR DESIGN, ATRIUM STEPHENSON BELL ARCHITECTS
STRUCTURAL AND CIVIL ENGINEER AMEC
SERVICES ENGINEER SHEPHERD ENGINEERING SERVICES
QS FAITHFUL & GOULD
CONTRACTOR ASTRAZENECA ENGINEERING
CONTRACT VALUE £65 MILLION
DATE OF COMPLETION OCTOBER 2005
GROSS INTERNAL AREA 20,000 SQUARE METRES
PHOTOGRAPHER DANIEL HOPKINSON

ARC
.HULL .NIALL MCLAUGHLIN ARCHITECTS

A challenging brief has led to a highly innovative moveable structure, flexible enough to accommodate a variety of cultural uses. The architecture is complemented by a series of renewable energy services that form a kind of technological artwork, symbolizing the importance of sustainable design, while at the same time reducing the running costs of the building. With Hull's history of caravan manufacturing, the technology and materials used are highly appropriate. The intention is to move Arc around the city as opportunities arise. But the structure makes other references, too: the lean-to is the most economical of forms – whether against a sea wall, or on an allotment – and Arc follows this simple design model.

The project delivers opportunities for the community to learn about the built environment in general and about their own city in particular. The building aims to reconnect Hull with its history and with the sea, on which it turned its back in the last century. So images of the sea and its changing moods are screened in real time.

Because Arc is a temporary installation and its use is flexible and open-ended, specific site influences and requirements have given way to issues of message, process and use. The building is therefore more a product or a piece of industrial design than architecture in the traditional sense. Nevertheless, it is witty and memorable and the internal space is dramatic and uplifting.

Detailing is simple and always expressive of the moveable quality of the building. Integration of services and structure is simple and effective. Although building sustainability and low energy use are major elements of the design (with biomass boiler, photovoltaic panels, wind turbines and passive cooling), they are used to complement the basic idea of the moveable object.

CLIENT THE ARC
STRUCTURAL ENGINEER PRICE & MYERS
SERVICES ENGINEER XCO2
QS E.C. HARRIS
CONTRACTOR WRIGHT CONSTRUCTION
CONTRACT VALUE £570,000
DATE OF COMPLETION JANUARY 2006
PHOTOGRAPHER NICK KANE

SHORTLISTED FOR THE RIBA SUSTAINABILITY AWARD

END ELEVATION

BROUGHTON HALL PAVILION
.SKIPTON .HOPKINS ARCHITECTS

Broughton Hall's new pavilion is an exquisite and finely tailored intervention in a historic walled garden. The building is rigorously detailed and constructed with a precision that resonates with its Zen-like intention. Beautifully understated, a simple roofplane defines the central function space, framed by symmetrical pods to the north and south. The detailing is similarly understated and benefits from the highest quality of materials and workmanship.

The result is sublime and complete, settling easily into the calm landscaping by Dan Pearson. This setting has been carefully considered, and the landscape will add to the sense of arrival as it matures. The building acts as a frame, giving uninterrupted views to and from a walled garden. It is an inside/outside space that gives all of its occupants a sense of ownership and fellowship. The classical symmetry of the plan creates a quiet calm that functions well as an escape for the various inhabitants of the estate offices.

The central common room incorporates frameless glass front and back, and is flanked by timber bookends that conceal the structural columns and contain the smaller rooms. Overhanging eaves support a veranda, providing shade and a place for tables and chairs.

Structure, building services and architecture are well considered and seamlessly put together. Looking deeper, there are surprising touches that add delight, such as the roof pond that makes the roof a mirror of the sky when seen from the surrounding landscape.

CLIENT BROUGHTON HALL BUSINESS PARK
STRUCTURAL ENGINEER BURO HAPPOLD
LANDSCAPE ARCHITECT DAN PEARSON STUDIO
CONTRACTORS BROUGHTON HALL ESTATE/ RURAL SOLUTIONS LTD
CONTRACT VALUE CONFIDENTIAL
DATE OF COMPLETION 2005
GROSS INTERNAL AREA 240 SQUARE METRES
PHOTOGRAPHER SIMON MILES

SHORTLISTED FOR THE STEPHEN LAWRENCE PRIZE

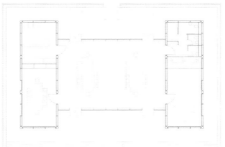

GROUND-FLOOR PLAN

UNDERGROUND GALLERY, YORKSHIRE SCULPTURE PARK .WAKEFIELD
.FEILDEN CLEGG BRADLEY ARCHITECTS

This gallery complements the previous phases of development at the Yorkshire Sculpture Park with an understated design that is the embodiment of elegance and simplicity. As an extension to the existing (and relatively new) visitor centre here, the underground gallery completes the building. It also provides a stronger sense of arrival in the park, as it forms the transition from car park and entrance to the landscape and its installations.

The building is so simple that it is almost invisible, but it is very carefully assembled from robust and beautiful materials. It responds to its setting so subtly that it does not ask any questions of its users. The work displayed in the gallery is given the prominence it deserves – not just unimpeded, but actually quietly enhanced by the architecture.

The gallery gives the client the versatile internal exhibition space that it needed. Three rooms can be opened into one 12-metre by 36-metre space, whose size can be increased still further by taking in the wide concourse. Lighting is computer-controlled, enabling moods to be created to suit changing exhibitions. Integration of structure and services is simple and robust. Unusually, natural ventilation is used for two-thirds of the gallery spaces, and the thermal mass of the exposed concrete construction is exploited to the maximum.

The site itself, the nineteenth-century Bothy Garden, is an especially difficult proposition, being a formal shell-shaped walled kitchen garden. Those who knew the place in its former incarnation must feel that the spirit of the newly created place is strong, unobtrusive, calm and appropriate.

CLIENT YORKSHIRE SCULPTURE PARK
STRUCTURAL ENGINEER WSP
SERVICES ENGINEER ERNEST GRIFFITHS
LANDSCAPING LAND USE CONSULTANTS
PROJECT MANAGER BURNLEY WILSON SMITH
CONTRACTOR QUARMBY CONSTRUCTION COMPANY LTD
CONTRACT VALUE £2.75 MILLION
DATE OF COMPLETION DECEMBER 2004
GROSS INTERNAL AREA 1056 SQUARE METRES
PHOTOGRAPHER JONTY WILDE

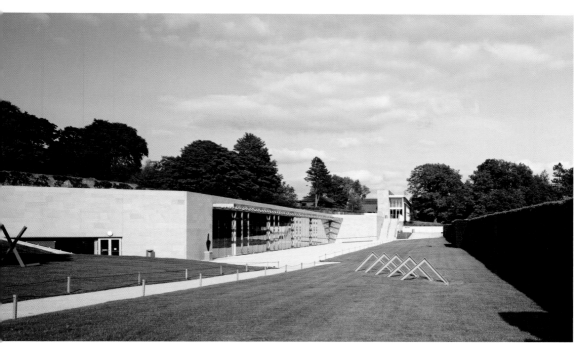

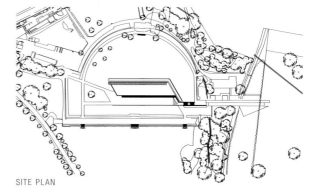

SITE PLAN

NATIONAL WATERFRONT MUSEUM
.SWANSEA .WILKINSON EYRE ARCHITECTS

One of the key aims of the brief was to create a free museum that would re-engage the public with a significant collection covering the culture and heritage of Wales. The waterfront site, which was occupied by a listed warehouse and originally traversed by a network of railway tracks, provided one of the bases for the regeneration of Swansea's Maritime Quarter. The architects clearly engaged with the site's history, retaining the warehouse as a series of controlled exhibition spaces, and forming a new contrasting open gallery that follows the arc of the original tracks in a series of interlocking stages. New and old are seamlessly linked by a foyer space.

Even more impressive than these formal gestures is the sense of democracy the building has brought to the idea of the museum; the curators' wish was to avoid the usual 'ramraiding visitors into understanding'. The Waterfront Museum is a place to meet, attracting casual visitors as well as serious museum-goers. The foyer is generous enough to allow varied and flexible information programmes as well as space in which people can linger and socialize.

A slate wall made up of precisely grouped riven-faced panels lines the southern aspect of the new building and relates to the fully glazed and stepped entry façade. Just as impressive is the seamless integration of virtual and physical displays in the converted warehouse building. The main exhibition space within this building has become very popular as a site for functions – providing a valuable income source for the museum – as its moveable cabinets can be reorganized without great effort.

The museum team is enthusiastic about the way the building is already engaging audiences from many quarters, and the architects have played a major part in this with the intelligence of their design.

CLIENT NATIONAL WATERFRONT MUSEUM SWANSEA
STRUCTURAL AND CIVIL ENGINEER ARUP
SERVICES ENGINEER MCCANN & PARTNERS
EXHIBITION DESIGNER LAND DESIGN STUDIO LTD
QS DAVIS LANGDON
CONTRACTOR MOWLEM
CONTRACT VALUE £15 MILLION
DATE OF COMPLETION NOVEMBER 2004
GROSS INTERNAL AREA 6080 SQUARE METRES
PHOTOGRAPHERS HÉLÈNE BINET/JAMES BRITTAIN (LEFT)

THE SPIRAL CAFÉ
.BIRMINGHAM .MARKS BARFIELD ARCHITECTS

This project demonstrates architecture's ability to enhance the quality and richness of the public realm, raising a smile as it does so. Architect and client have lifted the ordinary into the delightful. The programme for this tiny but strikingly sculptural building was simple enough: a small café located on a raised terrace directly overlooking both St Martin's Church and a water-sculpture cascade at the eastern edge of the new Bullring commercial district in Birmingham's city centre. But the result, situated at the faultline between the commercial and the spiritual areas of the city, is anything but commonplace.

Part sculpture, part architecture, the building form is inspired by the discoveries of Fibonacci, who, in the thirteenth century, identified mathematical patterns of natural growth from the shapes of seashells. This understanding has been ingeniously applied by the architects in an adventurous response to the challenge of providing a small freestanding building within this monumental and successful retail complex.

The building, a spiralling copper shell, hard and scaled on the outside in special pre-oxidized copper strips, and with lacquered shiny brass panels on the inside, completes the zoomorphic illusion. In a vigorous coup de théâtre the architects have wrapped the roof into the interior floor, so it curls upwards to reappear as the coffee-shop counter. This stunning invention draws the eye and entices the passer-by to enter.

Despite the complexity of its construction and its attention-seeking design, the building was not vandalized in its first eighteen months of active use, and the materials appear to be holding up well. On a per-square-metre rate the café is astonishingly expensive, but in the context of a major commercial development such as the Bullring this is almost incidental.

CLIENT HAMMERSON UK PROPERTIES PLC ON BEHALF OF THE BIRMINGHAM ALLIANCE
STRUCTURAL ENGINEER PRICE & MYERS 3D ENGINEERING
SERVICES ENGINEER WSP
CONTRACTOR THOMAS VALE
CONTRACT VALUE £650,000
DATE OF COMPLETION OCTOBER 2004
GROSS INTERNAL AREA 60 SQUARE METRES
PHOTOGRAPHER PETER DURANT

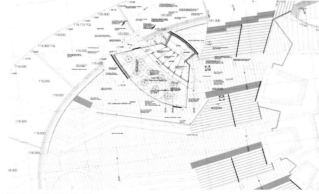

GROUND-FLOOR PLAN

13 .WEST MIDLANDS

THE COLLECTION, CITY AND COUNTY MUSEUM
.LINCOLN .PANTER HUDSPITH ARCHITECTS

In the historic heart of Lincoln, halfway up the hill on top of which the medieval cathedral sits, The Collection forms a part of the Flaxengate masterplan for a cultural quarter that seeks to regenerate the whole area. The new building works as a piece of urban design and as a museum and exhibition space. It is also a triumph of detailing and craftsmanship.

The building mass is broken down into five geologically inspired forms that are a direct response to the scale and character of the medieval city. These elements form a small public square, the hard landscaping of which also reflects the geological inspiration behind the building.

The Collection is entered from the north through a pavilion that contains a café and shop. The entire exterior is clad in Lincolnshire limestone, detailed using many forms and surface textures. The cave-like interior of the entrance pavilion is formed from board-faced self-compacting in-situ concrete that has been lovingly detailed and constructed. Both the shop and the café are delightful spaces that benefit from carefully framed views of the courtyard and the cathedral.

The main exhibition spaces are entered from a glass walkway into a central glass-roofed circulation area from which the temporary and permanent collections and auditorium are accessed. The main gallery spaces are flexible and have high-level north-facing rooflights that provide optimum lighting conditions for the exhibits. The conference and education rooms and staff offices have been as beautifully considered and detailed as the front-of-house facilities.

CLIENT THE COLLECTION
STRUCTURAL ENGINEER PRICE & MYERS
SERVICES ENGINEER ARUP
QS BURKE HUNTER ADAMS
CONTRACTOR CADDICK CONSTRUCTION
CONTRACT VALUE £7.8 MILLION
DATE OF COMPLETION OCTOBER 2005
GROSS INTERNAL AREA 4030 SQUARE METRES
PHOTOGRAPHER HÉLÈNE BINET

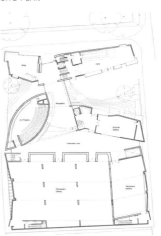

NORTHAMPTON ACADEMY .NORTHAMPTON .FEILDEN CLEGG BRADLEY ARCHITECTS

This is a new non-selective, non-fee-paying secondary school and sixth form for 1420 pupils. It replaces a school on a site on the edge of a wooded river valley, and was the subject of a number of constraints imposed by the Environment Agency. The school is formed from four linked pavilions housing individual subject bases to the south of a central courtyard, with the administration, school hall, entrance and gymnasium to its north. The pavilions are linked by circulation spaces at high level, allowing the courtyard to spread out to the south and connect with the river valley. This strategy is completely successful and achieves a synthesis between internal and external spaces.

The wide circulation spaces are monitored from glass-faced staff bases: in practice there is nowhere within the school that is unobserved by staff. This is not as uncomfortable as it sounds: the democratic nature of glass means that students can also observe staff in their bases. The naturally illuminated circulation routes vary in width and scale, acting also as valuable additional exhibition and work spaces. They give vitality and a sense of cohesion to the entire school and have the quality of an art gallery rather than a corridor in a secondary school.

The Northampton Academy inspires pupils and staff with a safe, stimulating and democratic environment in which to work. Coupled with excellent environmental credentials and fine detailing, the building has been delivered with quality and panache.

CLIENT ULT (UNITED LEARNING TRUST)
ENGINEER BURO HAPPOLD
LANDSCAPE ARCHITECT PLINCKE LANDSCAPE
QS CM PARKER BROWNE
CONTRACTOR MILLER CONSTRUCTION
CONTRACT VALUE £19.5 MILLION
DATE OF COMPLETION MARCH 2006
GROSS INTERNAL AREA 12,480 SQUARE METRES
PHOTOGRAPHER PETER COOK – VIEW

NORTHAMPTON ACADEMY WAS REVISITED BY THE RIBA AWARDS GROUP AND CONSIDERED FOR THE STIRLING SHORTLIST

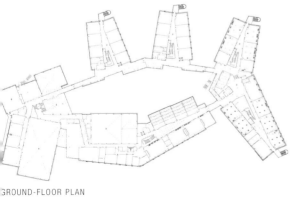

GROUND-FLOOR PLAN

VISITOR CENTRE, ATTENBOROUGH NATURE RESERVE
.NOTTINGHAM .GROUNDWORKS ARCHITECTS

The building is located on a 157-hectare Site of Special Scientific Interest (SSSI), a nature reserve formed from disued gravel workings on the urban fringe of Nottingham. The challenge was to provide Nottinghamshire Wildlife Trust with a flagship sustainable building providing open and flexible facilities to include visitor orientation and education, catering, shop and toilets, and a base for permanent staff and volunteers.

It was decided to locate the building on a small peninsula jutting into one of the main lakes, the shoremost edge of the peninsula being cut through to transform it into an island. The centre is entered across a causeway, which is raised on concrete piles above the one-in-one-hundred-year flood level. The linear theme continues in the form of an east–west spine, with accommodation on either side making the best of the views of the landscape and wildlife while giving the best possible opportunity for passive and active solar collection. The building is secured, when it is not being used, with a drawbridge; when raised this makes a formidable vandal-proof barrier.

Using materials from sustainable sources, local contractors and suppliers were involved wherever possible. Intelligent use is made of active sustainable energy-generation techniques: a heat exchanger employs lake water to warm the building, and photovoltaic panels harvest solar energy, providing significant quantities of electricity. The building is designed to have a low-to-neutral carbon footprint, which would have been achieved in practice but for the unexpectedly high number of visitors.

The way the centre floats above the lake is a joy. The roof form, although derived from function, is reminiscent of a bird in flight, adding to the sense of delight.

CLIENT NOTTINGHAMSHIRE WILDLIFE TRUST
ENGINEER PRICE & MYERS
ENVIRONMENTAL CONSULTANT LEEDS ENVIRONMENTAL DESIGN ASSOCIATES
QS APPLEYARD AND TREW LLP
CONTRACTOR LOACH CONSTRUCTION
CONTRACT VALUE £1.3 MILLION
DATE OF COMPLETION MARCH 2005
GROSS INTERNAL AREA 410 SQUARE METRES
PHOTOGRAPHER MARTINE HAMILTON KNIGHT

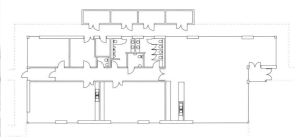

GROUND-FLOOR PLAN

GIRTON COLLEGE LIBRARY AND ARCHIVE
.CAMBRIDGE .ALLIES AND MORRISON

At Girton – the women's college – the architects have achieved an extraordinarily difficult piece of integration, providing new library facilities in an uncompromisingly modern style in a neo-Gothic setting. The building resorts to neither pastiche nor gimmick, although there are echoes of the best twentieth-century work from Scandinavia and Japan.

The brief called for a design that would provide environmentally stable conditions for Girton's archives, without air conditioning. The tough challenge would have been relished by the college's original architect, Alfred Waterhouse, whose massive ventilation chimneys at the Natural History Museum in London bear witness to his early attempts to do something similar. Allies and Morrison's solution is based on the principle of two separated boxes, one inside the other: the inner one a heavy masonry structure, the outer one with brick walls and a heavy lead roof.

The extension, containing a reading room, staff facilities, meeting rooms, rare-document archives and a book-restoration workshop, is arranged in an L-shaped plan. There is an almost seamless transition between old and new, with each detail lovingly honed. The quality of light internally is extraordinary. Outside, a beautiful secluded courtyard, overlooked by the reading room but almost invisible from the college grounds, has been created by borrowing the side of the chapel and adding the two wings of the new building.

This is a well-loved building providing memorable internal and external spaces. It elicits a very enthusiastic response from client and users, who now have easy access to the remarkable collections previously housed in boxes in corridors and offices.

CLIENT GIRTON COLLEGE
STRUCTURAL ENGINEER WHITBYBIRD
SERVICES ENGINEER ATELIER TEN
QS SHERIFF TIPLADY ASSOCIATES
CONTRACTOR BLUESTONE PLC
CONTRACT VALUE £1.6 MILLION
DATE OF COMPLETION APRIL 2005
GROSS INTERNAL AREA 400 SQUARE METRES
PHOTOGRAPHER DENNIS GILBERT – VIEW

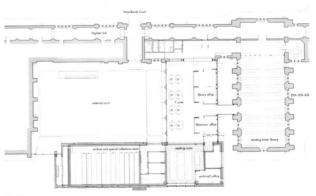

PLAN

BREWHOUSE AND CLARENCE BUILDINGS .PLYMOUTH .ACANTHUS FERGUSON MANN ARCHITECTS

The Grade I-listed Royal William Yard had long been a wonderful but unfulfilled development opportunity. Then the Plymouth Development Corporation carried out the base restoration, taking some of the risk out of the equation. This initial conservation work was undertaken by Gilmore Hankey Kirke. At this point Manchester-based Urban Splash were persuaded to bring their special expertise and commitment to design quality to the south-west.

They have created a mixed-use development in the Brewhouse, with an arts facility, café and restaurant on the quayside ground floor, and with residential units in the rest of the building. The former general store, the Clarence Building, is all residential, and includes two triplexes that incorporate major granite staircases. The Brewhouse is organized around the huge (but never used) brewing hall. This generously continues an Urban Splash fire strategy and produces flats with extraordinary views.

The genius of the development and its design lies in Acanthus Ferguson Mann's understanding of the scale of the former Navy Victualling Yard built by Sir John Rennie in the 1820s; for this scheme to work it was essential that the accommodation was at a scale appropriate to the buildings, and it is. Big flats in big buildings are new to the south-west, but once again Urban Splash have picked the right architects and made their own market. Client and architect have pulled off a highly sophisticated act, developing a spectacularly simple vocabulary with huge but exquisitely simple matt stainless-steel and white kitchens, vast bathrooms (but then there is so much space to be used) and delightful look-no-detail doors.

CLIENT URBAN SPLASH
ASSOCIATED ARCHITECT GILMORE HANKEY KIRKE (ENVELOPE REPAIR)
STRUCTURAL ENGINEER ALAN BAXTER & ASSOCIATES
SERVICES ENGINEER FULCRUM CONSULTING
FIRE CONSULTANT INTERNATIONAL FIRE CONSULTANTS
PLANNING SUPERVISOR HYDER CONSULTING
ACOUSTIC CONSULTANT NOISE.CO.UK
QS DAVIS LANGDON
CONTRACTOR MIDAS PROJECTS UK LTD
CONTRACT VALUE £15 MILLION
DATE OF COMPLETION JUNE 2005
GROSS INTERNAL AREA 16,187 SQUARE METRES
PHOTOGRAPHER TREVOR BURROWS

LEVEL 2 PLAN

THE DEVON GUILD OF CRAFTSMEN
.BOVEY TRACEY .SOFTROOM

In 1986 a group of craftsmen who had been exhibiting in Devon since the 1950s bought the coach-house of a pub hemmed in by a fast-flowing river, the pub's car park and a road. Behind a high wall the U-shaped building provided space for a café, but the main exhibition space was relatively inaccessible at first-floor level. Spurred on by the Lottery and with generous funds from other public bodies too, they have now built a large ground-floor gallery with the café terrace on its roof, allowing the first-floor café, accessible by lift, to double as a meeting and lecture room.

Chosen by the client through a mini-competition, the architect has created a stunning gallery in which the ceiling is swept up like a magic carpet to float over the wall that defines the courtyard; this is held on the daintiest stub columns imaginable. To make the most of every square metre of space on a tight site, an old staircase has been reconfigured, reusing the original granite treads. The sedum-planted roof accommodates a comfortable timber deck terrace for the café. Full-height sliding oak doors connect the gallery with the courtyard, so that exhibits can spill outside when the weather allows.

The design is inspired by the kind of temporary structures made by slinging a canvas roof across the tops of two walls. Here the roof is a slender steel construct, rising towards the north to allow rooflights to admit the best viewing light into the gallery below.

This is a stimulating and engaging spatial experience. And, at a little under half a million pounds, it represents great value for the guild.

CLIENT DEVON GUILD OF CRAFTSMEN
STRUCTURAL ENGINEER TECHNIKER
ARTIST MARTIN RICHMAN
QS JAMES NISBET & PARTNERS
CONTRACTOR ROK GROUP PLC
CONTRACT VALUE £500,000
DATE OF COMPLETION SEPTEMBER 2004
GROSS INTERNAL AREA 150 SQUARE METRES
PHOTOGRAPHER JOSEPH BURNS

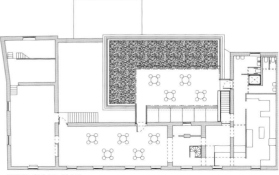

FIRST-FLOOR PLAN

BLAISE CASTLE CAFÉ
.BRISTOL .CODA ARCHITECTS

This is a carefully considered and necessarily robust solution to a nationwide problem to which good design is all too seldom seen as relevant: vandalism. The project is for local-authority public toilets, with a small office in one wing and a café in the other, set on the edge of an open public park within a listed Repton landscape and adjacent to a Grade II*-listed house. The café and toilets are part of a Heritage Lottery-funded restoration scheme for the park and part of the house.

The building shelters behind the retained wall of a historic barn. On the approach a water-wall engages people of all ages. The toilets have smart, robust details and are protected by heavy timber and stainless-steel doors that swing shut over the lobbies at night, and open by day to cover the rendered walls so that any graffiti is out of sight. The toilets have underfloor heating to cure the curse of condensation that besets most outside facilities.

The café is protected by great wedge-wire screens that swing out at right angles by day to form bays; sliding glazed doors open in summer to connect inside to out. The high projecting stainless-steel eaves are curved to discourage climbing on to the flattish roofs.

This is a sophisticated exercise in designing vandalism out: every detail was worked out with the committed client, himself a landscape architect. Procured outside the straitjacket of council procedures, the client has got exactly what he wanted: an open and free space by day, Fort Knox by night.

CLIENT BRISTOL CITY COUNCIL
STRUCTURAL ENGINEER INTEGRAL STRUCTURAL DESIGN
SERVICES CONSULTANT HALCROW LTD
LANDSCAPE ARCHITECT 4DLD
CONTRACTOR STRADFORM
CONTRACT VALUE £624,000
DATE OF COMPLETION MARCH 2005
GROSS INTERNAL AREA 150 SQUARE METRES
PHOTOGRAPHER JOAKIN BORÉN

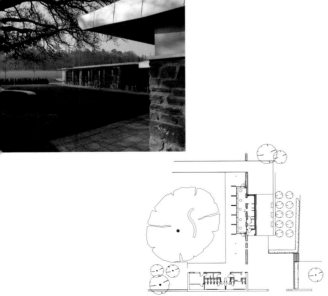

SITE PLAN

THE EGG
.BATH .HAWORTH TOMPKINS

The Egg is the third and smallest performance space for the Theatre Royal Bath. This delightful small-scale children's theatre has been inserted into the shell of a former parish hall, latterly used as a cinema. Not only is the building Grade II-listed, but the whole city is also a UNESCO World Heritage Site. Necessarily, therefore, the Bath stone exterior has been left untouched save for restoration, and the remains of the interiors have been left as found when exposed, following the insertion of the new performance space. The raking steel structure holds together the original fabric without touching the foundations. Further planning constraints included the need for added sound insulation on thin party walls, and a convoluted fire-escape strategy involving the adjoining theatres.

The brief was developed with a group of children as a piece of theatre. They continue to work on future programming. The structure is supported on raking columns standing low over an open, child-scaled entrance café, which is particularly popular with mothers and small children.

The main theatre seats 125 children on two levels and is fully accessible, with wheelchair-accessible lighting gantries above. The backdrop is the inner face of the front façade. The outer walls of the egg-shaped performance space are made of red felt-covered padded bolsters to protect both the building and excitable children. Low viewing windows are cut into it, and, for the more challenging young people, there is a time-out space that looks down into the theatre.

The project is full of carefully detailed child-centred incident. The top floor has a flexible studio and green room with a tiny terrace overlooking the roofs of Bath, and the basement houses toilets and a workshop.

CLIENT THEATRE ROYAL BATH
STRUCTURAL AND SERVICES ENGINEER BURO HAPPOLD
QS BURO HAPPOLD
THEATRE CONSULTANT AMPC
ACOUSTICS CONSULTANT FLEMING & BARRON
CONTRACTOR EMERYS OF BATH
CONTRACT VALUE £2.3 MILLION
DATE OF COMPLETION OCTOBER 2005
GROSS INTERNAL AREA 854 SQUARE METRES
PHOTOGRAPHER PHILIP VILE

SHORTLISTED FOR THE CROWN ESTATE CONSERVATION AWARD AND FOR THE RIBA INCLUSIVE DESIGN AWARD

THE EGG WAS REVISITED BY THE RIBA AWARDS GROUP AND CONSIDERED FOR THE STIRLING SHORTLIST

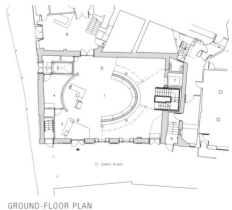

ST JOHN'S PLACE

GROUND-FLOOR PLAN

129 .WESSEX

NEW TEACHING AND ADMINISTRATION BUILDINGS, BEDALES SCHOOL
.PETERSFIELD .WALTERS AND COHEN

Bedales School comes from the confluence of two of the early twentieth century's greatest movements: socialism and Arts and Crafts. This spirit inspires Walters and Cohen's new heart for the school, the teaching and administration buildings that are the first part of a new masterplan. The architects were chosen following a competition that eliminated such impressive names as Niall McLaughlin, Glenn Howells and dRMM.

The architects took part in the Department of Education and Skills's Schools for the Future competition in 2003: working with Max Fordham and Adams Kara Taylor (both of whom also collaborated on Bedales), they looked at ways in which schools could be made more energy-efficient and in which the traditional breakdown between classrooms and circulation routes could be rethought. Here at Bedales they have applied the theoretical lessons to make a well-detailed addition to the school that functions successfully for teachers and students. The intelligent control of the external environment creates well-lit classrooms, while robust detailing gives the building a relaxed atmosphere that is particularly appropriate to the school's teaching philosophy.

In keeping with the local design guide, the scheme takes the form of two barn-like structures of three storeys, linked by a two-storey building with roof terrace. The classrooms face north to avoid the effects of solar gain, and they are naturally ventilated; on the south side are the top-lit circulation areas. This is a highly specified but not indulgent scheme, and a highly sustainable one – costing considerably less per square metre than schools in the City Academies Programme.

CLIENT BEDALES SCHOOL
STRUCTURAL ENGINEER ADAMS KARA TAYLOR
SERVICES ENGINEER MAX FORDHAM LLP
LANDSCAPE ARCHITECT EDWARD HUTCHISON LANDSCAPE ARCHITECTS
QS FANSHAWE
CONTRACTOR R. DURTNELL & SONS LTD
CONTRACT VALUE £7.5 MILLION
DATE OF OCCUPATION AUGUST 2005
GROSS INTERNAL AREA 3900 SQUARE METRES
PHOTOGRAPHER DENNIS GILBERT – VIEW

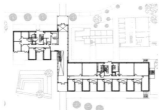

GROUND-FLOOR PLAN

NEW TERMINAL/OPERATIONS BUILDING
.FARNBOROUGH .REID ARCHITECTURE

The TAG (Techniques d'Avant Garde) group is developing Farnborough Airport for business aviation. The architects were given the following brief: 'The new terminal will constitute the flagship building and must represent the TAG image within aviation and must meet the needs of all TAG's business aviation customers, including travellers and the range of companies that will be resident at the site providing a range of business aviation services.'

The architects' response is a wing floating over the landscape. It is a highly sculptural building: long and narrow but cranked in the middle, finished (appropriately for a building handling aircraft) in aluminium shingles. The wing encloses a curved tube of space that links the north and south entrances in a triple-height reception area. All passenger facilities are on the largely glazed ground floor. Offices on the floor above have access to terraces at either end of the building.

The architects have managed to create an innovative and high-end building without a high-end budget – the project was delivered through a design-and-build route and is none the worse for it. The intelligent use of the shingle-cladding system copes with the dynamic form of the building; it is both well detailed and appropriate to its context, the building users and the client. The internal spaces are well arranged with excellent natural daylighting throughout. The location of windows relates the internal spaces to the airfield beyond.

CLIENT TAG FARNBOROUGH AIRPORT
STRUCTURAL AND SERVICES ENGINEER BURO HAPPOLD
LANDSCAPE ARCHITECT LOVEJOY
QS CYRIL SWEETT
CONTRACTOR TAG CONSTRUCTION MANAGEMENT
CONTRACT VALUE £10.2 MILLION
DATE OF OCCUPATION JANUARY 2006
GROSS INTERNAL AREA 4570 SQUARE METRES
PHOTOGRAPHER NICK HUFTON (HUFTON + CROW)

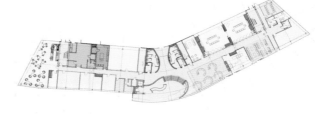

GROUND-FLOOR PLAN

PINIONS BARN
.HIGHAM CROSS, BUCKINGHAMSHIRE .SIMON CONDER ASSOCIATES

This conversion of two linear stone barns into a weekend retreat succeeds in raising the ubiquitous 'barn conversion' to a new level. The two structures are kept as simple, discrete blocks defining a wedge-shaped courtyard between them. One barn contains the principal living spaces and bedrooms, while the second provides separate accommodation for the offspring.

The approach to the conversion is clear and effective. Internally, new partitions, floors and fittings are treated almost as furniture, spaced away from the existing envelope. Stone walls have been ingeniously lined with a thick plywood skin that provides thermal insulation, lighting, and recesses concealing storage for books, sound systems and TV. The lining also adds to the impression of a massive structure by visually doubling the thickness of the wall seen at each opening.

Externally, the buildings reinterpret the traditional barn language of narrow openings in new ways. There are only three exceptions to the principle of reusing existing openings for doors and windows, and these give the scheme its striking character. The existing pattern of vertical slots is dramatically reversed, with one long horizontal slot window running parallel to the kitchen work surface, giving protracted views of trains sliding past a field away. A full-height vertical window allows north light to flood into the barn. And, finally, the east-facing wall of the smaller barn has been removed completely, opening up the living space to the valley below. None of the windows is openable – air is drawn in through vents in pivoting timber panels – so the glass could be inserted into the stone without visible frames, emphasizing the massiveness of the walls.

The building is both innovative and daring, yet it remains understated. As a result it transforms the existing structures without undermining their quality.

CLIENT WILLIAM ECCLESHARE
STRUCTURAL ENGINEER BUILT STRUCTURAL ENGINEERING LTD
CONTRACTOR HERBERT AUSTIN LTD
CONTRACT VALUE £656,000
DATE OF OCCUPATION SEPTEMBER 2004
GROSS INTERNAL AREA 378 SQUARE METRES
PHOTOGRAPHER CHRIS GASCOIGNE – VIEW

SHORTLISTED FOR THE CROWN ESTATE CONSERVATION AWARD AND FOR THE STEPHEN LAWRENCE PRIZE

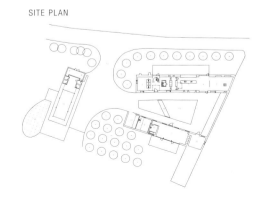

ST CATHERINE'S COLLEGE, PHASE 2
.OXFORD .HODDER ASSOCIATES

The architects have managed to create a sensitive addition to the campus of Arne Jacobsen buildings, previously added to by Stephen Hodder in 1994. The new work, while being of a piece with the original masterplan, has a style of its own. The architects are thus following in a tradition of evolutionary development, a design principle that underlies everything that happens in the college.

Phase 2 comprises 132 study-bedrooms with en-suite shower rooms, built around the traditional Oxbridge staircase, a porter's lodge and four teaching rooms. Half of the bedrooms and the porter's lodge line up with the west-facing Jacobsen wing, while most of the other rooms are aligned north–south; only the ends of the blocks are turned through 90 degrees, allowing a protective cloister to be extended throughout the scheme. The staircases and pantries are glazed to give views of Music Meadow and Headington.

Internal spaces are of an exceptionally high quality, and there is a clear and intelligent arrangement of both the public and the private areas within the residential accommodation.

At the laying of the foundation stone of the original college buildings in 1960 Arne Jacobsen said, 'I have used concrete but only for the bearing structure. For the finishes I rely on natural materials which weather with beautiful patinas and that is why I have made use of brick …. They give a human scale and unity to the whole college.' Hodder's work speaks the same language – only the idiom is different and of the twenty-first century.

CLIENT FELLOWS OF ST CATHERINE'S COLLEGE, OXFORD
STRUCTURAL ENGINEER SKM ANTHONY HUNTS
SERVICES ENGINEER MAX FORDHAM
QS NORTHCROFT
CONTRACTOR GALLIFORD TRY CONSTRUCTION LTD
CONTRACT VALUE £8.7 MILLION
DATE OF OCCUPATION OCTOBER 2004/ JANUARY 2005
GROSS INTERNAL AREA 4274 SQUARE METRES
PHOTOGRAPHER MARTINE HAMILTON KNIGHT

SENIOR COMMON ROOM, ST JOHN'S COLLEGE
.OXFORD .MACCORMAC JAMIESON PRICHARD

It is never easy to work in the context of a Grade I-listed building, especially in the centre of a historic city like Oxford, but here MacCormac Jamieson Prichard have pulled it off with their customary tact and sensitivity.

This project extends the existing senior common room building, which dates from 1676. This is landscape design as much as architecture, the aim being to introduce the existing gardens to the new building and vice versa. The result is a series of contemplative indoor and outdoor spaces.

The design provides new sitting rooms, a roof terrace and an extended lunch-room on the first floor. It takes the form of a two-storey glass box cantilevered over the garden. Oak louvres on a steel-and-oak frame reflect the surrounding treescape. The new concrete frame sits on piled foundations so no loads are added to ancient buildings. Rooms in the existing building have been remodelled to provide disabled access in line with current legislation. This involved the delicate insertion of two new platform lifts.

The architects have managed to maintain a clear concept for the building from design to completion, creating a sensitive and cohesive addition to the college. The context is extremely complicated, but the extension manages to fuse the various earlier additions into a satisfying whole, while creating distinctive new spaces. The use of electrically operated timber louvres to transform the main dining space and its links to the garden beyond give the building an enjoyable sense of play and dynamism.

CLIENT ST JOHN'S COLLEGE, OXFORD
STRUCTURAL ENGINEER PRICE & MYERS
SERVICES ENGINEER BURO HAPPOLD
QS PETER GITTINS & ASSOCIATES
CONTRACTOR KINGERLEE LTD
CONTRACT VALUE CONFIDENTIAL
DATE OF OCCUPATION JULY 2004
GROSS INTERNAL AREA 90 SQUARE METRES
PHOTOGRAPHER PETER DURANT

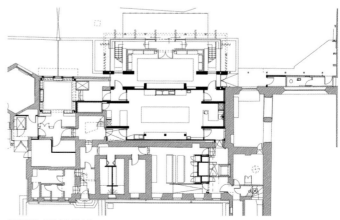

GROUND-FLOOR PLAN

ESHER HOUSE
.ESHER .WILKINSON KING ARCHITECTS

The brief called for a five-bedroom house with a good relationship between internal spaces. It was to be built on the site of the clients' old house, which architects, clients and planning authority agreed was long past the end of its useful life. The architects modestly describe this house as a box, but its design provides a masterful and spatially rich solution at a very significant level of excellence.

The building is well positioned on the site, with a punchy plan based on simple concepts that belie its richness and sophistication. The experience of spaces and the relationships between them as you move around are heightened by the generosity of light, the lofty ceilings and the carefully controlled views.

With its restrained materials palette, this is one of those rare projects to which you could add nothing, and from which nothing could be taken away. This is partly due to the patience of the clients, who were not prepared to sacrifice quality for speed of construction. The work was therefore phased, the first phase being the structure and envelope, the second the fit-out, and the third the landscaping and pool. The strategy has paid off.

The antecedents of the house are clear – Le Corbusier via Moro – but this is far from a pastiche. There is a confidence about the design, a crispness in the detailing and a panache about the delivery that mean that this building should still look excellent in thirty years. In the best modernist tradition, this house is all about light and shade; both are manipulated with consummate skill by the architects, for whom this is, remarkably, the first stand-alone building. Had the RIBA not abandoned its First Building Award this year, Esher House would surely have walked it.

CLIENTS DANIEL AND ANGELA MOK
STRUCTURAL ENGINEER PACKMAN LUCAS
QS COOK AND BUTLER
CONTRACTORS SWIFT SOUTHERN LTD (PHASE 1, ENVELOPE AND SUBSTRUCTURE)/ODB CONTRACTS LTD (PHASES 2 AND 3, FIT-OUT AND POOL WORKS)
CONTRACT VALUE £1.6 MILLION
DATE OF OCCUPATION JULY 2004
GROSS INTERNAL AREA 448 SQUARE METRES
PHOTOGRAPHER PAUL TYAGI – VIEW

SHORTLISTED FOR THE MANSER MEDAL

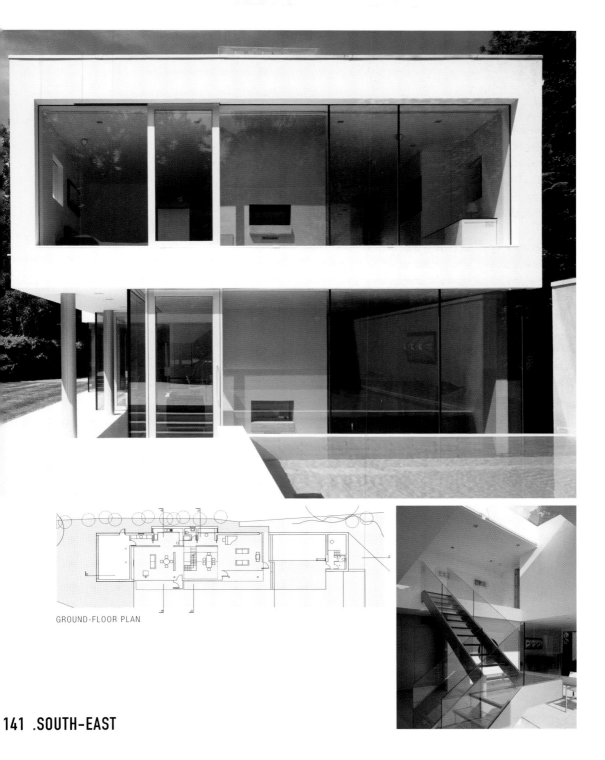

GROUND-FLOOR PLAN

HARBOUR MEADOW
.CHICHESTER .AVANTI ARCHITECTS

This is an immaculate restoration of a Grade II-listed but nevertheless severely deteriorated building, a wonderful house originally designed by Peter Moro and Richard Llewelyn in the late 1930s and completed shortly after the outbreak of war. It was Moro's first UK project and we owe it a lot, as he claimed that the job stopped him being deported. Without it, there would have been no Nottingham Playhouse.

The restoration has uncovered and rediscovered most of the house's original features and details. New interventions are sensitive and appropriate to the character of a fine building. Where materials were too damaged to be retrieved or repaired, the architects have provided suitable and sensitive alternatives that add to, rather than detract from, the original building.

Repairs included replacing all the roof coverings and reinstating a distinctive rooftop screen. Brick surfaces have been repaired and repainted in their original colours. Other lost colours – the pale-blue soffits and chocolate-brown garden re-entrant – have also been reproduced. Windows and doors had been almost wholly and unsympathetically replaced at an earlier stage; finer and thermally insulated replacements have been made. Throughout, the concrete and surviving original metalwork have been restored. The trick has been to make very little of this visible to the untutored eye.

This is clearly an excellent piece of conservation and a highly successful restoration of an architecturally significant building. It is also an extremely appropriate response to the brief, demonstrating high standards of research and analysis, which the completed landscape should complement.

CLIENTS LOUISE AND GORDON LAWSON
STRUCTURAL ENGINEER CAMPBELL REITH HILL
SERVICES CONSULTANT MARTIN THOMAS ASSOCIATES
QS BOXALL SAYER
PROJECT MANAGEMENT SMITHS GORE
CONTRACTOR E.A. CHIVERTON LTD
CONTRACT VALUE £1.8 MILLION
DATE OF OCCUPATION DECEMBER 2005
GROSS INTERNAL AREA 644 SQUARE METRES
PHOTOGRAPHER NICK KANE

SHORTLISTED FOR THE CROWN ESTATE CONSERVATION AWARD

THE MENUHIN HALL
.LEATHERHEAD .BURRELL FOLEY FISCHER

This building has been delivered on an exceptionally tight budget but is none the poorer for that. Set in the greenbelt and within earshot of the M25, the hall is conspicuously located (behind an acoustic barrier of mature trees) in a prominent position on a site that slopes gently away from the loose collection of school buildings that is strung along the skyline.

The hall seats 316 and has a platform to accommodate up to 45 musicians. Externally, it is simple, economical and restrained. A glazed timber structure confidently wraps around the brick- and zinc-clad hall, masking its scale. Inside, the hall is magic in maple. The acoustics are remarkable: designed to be 'supportive', they are boosted so that singers and instrumentalists do not have to strain to fill the space. In this way the hall bridges the huge gap for students between the small-scale rehearsal and performance spaces elsewhere in the school and the vast volumes of world-class auditoria. Everything from the stage approach to the backstage areas is direct and sensitive to the needs of young performers, making this a remarkably flexible and friendly performance building.

From the first impression on entering the grounds through to the footpath approach down the winding path, the straightforward L-shaped foyer and sensuous interior of the hall, this project exudes straightforward quality, confidence and pragmatism. It is an exemplary instance of a great client working with an excellent architect to come up with a very clear and consummate design.

CLIENT THE YEHUDI MENUHIN SCHOOL
STRUCTURAL ENGINEER MICHAEL BARCLAY PARTNERSHIP
SERVICES CONSULTANT MICHAEL POPPER ASSOCIATES
ACOUSTIC CONSULTANT SOUND SPACE DESIGN
PERFORMANCE CONSULTANT ANNE MINORS PERFORMANCE CONSULTANTS
QS DAVIS LANGDON LLP
CONTRACTOR R DURTNELL & SONS LTD
CONTRACT VALUE £2.8 MILLION
DATE OF OCCUPATION OCTOBER 2005
PHOTOGRAPHER DENNIS GILBERT — VIEW

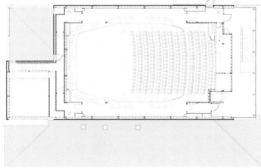

FIRST-FLOOR
PLAN

CHRIST CHURCH SPITALFIELDS .LONDON E1 .PURCELL MILLER TRITTON WITH WILLIAM WHITFIELD AND PARTNERS

Christ Church in Spitalfields was designed by Nicholas Hawksmoor on the scale of a small cathedral and built between 1714 and 1729. However, it has been altered several times during its history, including the removal of its galleries and box pews in 1866 and the lowering of its window cills in the late nineteenth century. By 1957 the church was nearly derelict and services were held elsewhere. In 1976 the Friends of Christ Church Spitalfields was formed, primarily to restore the building and bring it back to use. The finished project is the result of thirty years of restoration.

The seamless internal restoration complements the external fabric, which was cleaned and restored in the 1990s. The interior stone and plasterwork is painted in shades of white and off-white, giving an impression of cleanliness and beauty. The galleries have been reinstated at first-floor level in what could only be described as a thirty-year labour of love – the architect Andrew 'Red' Mason had retained all the antique joinery for use in restoration. He also located the grease marks left by the handprints of the congregation at an intermediate level of the giant columns in order to establish the exact position of the gallery fascia.

A decision has been made not to restore the box pews, and the congregation sits instead on moveable chairs – allowing the nave to be used in several ways and providing valuable income for the restoration fund. (Additional funding for this scrupulous, tasteful and well-judged restoration has come from a variety of sources: the Heritage Lottery Fund, English Heritage, the World Monument Fund and The Monument Trust.) This is a lovingly researched and meticulously carried out piece of conservation; all the architects who have brought this remarkable church back to life are to be commended.

CLIENT FRIENDS OF CHRIST CHURCH SPITALFIELDS
STRUCTURAL ENGINEER HOCKLEY & DAWSON
SERVICES ENGINEER HILSON MORAN PARTNERSHIP
QS THE COOK & BUTLER PARTNERSHIP
CONTRACTOR WALLIS SPECIAL PROJECTS DIVISION
CONTRACT VALUE £4.7 MILLION
DATE OF COMPLETION AUGUST 2004
GROSS INTERNAL AREA 1100 SQUARE METRES
PHOTOGRAPHER S.R.B. HUMPHREYS

SHORTLISTED FOR THE CROWN ESTATE CONSERVATION AWARD

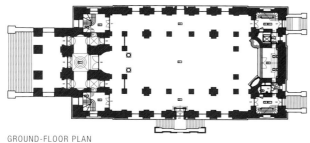

GROUND-FLOOR PLAN

THE DAVIES ALPINE HOUSE, ROYAL BOTANIC GARDENS, KEW
.RICHMOND .WILKINSON EYRE ARCHITECTS

The mature landscape of the Royal Botanic Gardens at Kew provides an enviable setting for any new building, but with that advantage comes a responsibility to provide a structure worthy of its context. Furthermore, this is an opportunity that does not fall to many architects, as the Davies Alpine House is the first new greenhouse at Kew for twenty years.

This solution to the problem of modifying the microclimate to serve the extraordinary variety of alpine plants is simple, elegant and very much up to the task. And it is bold. Wilkinson Eyre has rejected the safe option that would have tempted many building in a World Heritage Site; instead they have produced a greenhouse with the same spirit of ingenuity and innovation that imbued its predecessors.

A glass-clad symmetrical steel structure sits on a curved concrete base that accommodates a labyrinth of ducts blowing cooled air over the plants, reproducing the conditions in their native habitats. The structure has to be high enough to induce a stack effect, with cool air drawn in at low level, rising as it gets warmer and vented out at the top. Overhead lamps supplement the intensity of daylight, while two magical fan-shaped giant sails are operated to cover the inside of the entire glass surface and provide shade when needed.

For a small building, this is a powerful form. It is beautifully made and the synthesis of structure, surface and environmental control provides an enclosure worthy of the history of great botanical structures at Kew.

CLIENT ROYAL BOTANIC GARDENS, KEW
STRUCTURAL ENGINEER DEWHURST MACFARLANE & PARTNERS
SERVICES ENGINEER ATELIER TEN
GREENHOUSE ENGINEER GREEN-MARK INTERNATIONAL
QS FANSHAWE
CONTRACTORS TUCHSCHMID CONSTRUCTRA AG/KILLBY & GAYFORD
CONTRACT VALUE £850,000
DATE OF COMPLETION MAY 2005
GROSS INTERNAL AREA 144 SQUARE METRES
PHOTOGRAPHERS WILKINSON EYRE ARCHITECTS (MAIN PICTURE)/ NICK GUTTRIDGE

ALSO SHORTLISTED FOR THE STEPHEN LAWRENCE PRIZE

ROYAL BOTANIC GARDENS WAS THE RIBA/ARTS COUNCIL ENGLAND CLIENT OF THE YEAR

THE DAVIES ALPINE HOUSE WAS REVISITED BY THE RIBA AWARDS GROUP AND CONSIDERED FOR THE STIRLING SHORTLIST

DONNYBROOK QUARTER
.LONDON E3 .PETER BARBER ARCHITECTS

Donnybrook Quarter is the result of a winning entry in a competition run by Circle 33 Housing Association for housing that is flexible over time. To the enormous credit of both client and architect, the fresh vision of the original design comes through in the final scheme. It is a project that takes some of the assumptions of a typical social-housing scheme and asks difficult questions. Why should everyone not have the right to their own front door? Why doesn't housing contribute to the urban scene? What is the future of the street in the twenty-first century? How might one provide a slackness of space that can be appropriated over time?

The architects and client have come up with an answer that challenges many norms. The first sight of Donnybrook is almost shocking, with all that white amid the drabness of the East End. But the scheme is much more than an aesthetic game; it even plays with massing and composition in a skilful manner. The street that cuts through it is unlike anything recently built in the UK, being playful and full of potential for social exchange: balconies, bay windows and terraces all animate a place that recalls the best that a street might offer.

Termed a 'Mediterranean village' by the architectural press, with its wide open walkways and white buildings, Donnybrook Quarter uses the edges of the buildings to celebrate the public life of the street. While some may carp at rooms being entered directly from the street, the pay-off is that less of the scheme is given over to circulation and every flat and house has a private outside space.

While modernist in its hope and aesthetic, the scheme is decidedly unmodernist in its willingness to allow urban dwellers to take over and use its spaces in an undetermined manner. Its real triumph is in the spaces it creates and the social life that it may encourage. It is not a template to be rolled out for all housing schemes, but a project that should inspire others to think hard and innovatively about how we should design housing.

CLIENT CIRCLE ANGLIA LTD
ENGINEER COLIN TOMS & PARTNERS
QS LONDON BOROUGH OF WALTHAM FOREST SURVEYING DEPARTMENT
CONTRACTOR WILLMOTT DIXON
CONTRACT VALUE £4.5 MILLION
DATE OF COMPLETION JANUARY 2006
GROSS INTERNAL AREA 2618 SQUARE METRES
PHOTOGRAPHER MORLEY VON STERNBERG

DONNYBROOK WAS REVISITED BY THE RIBA AWARDS GROUP AND CONSIDERED FOR THE STIRLING SHORTLIST

GROUND-FLOOR PLAN

GAGOSIAN GALLERY, BRITANNIA STREET .LONDON WC1 .CARUSO ST JOHN ARCHITECTS

This building in Britannia Street, near King's Cross Station, formerly accommodated municipal garages. The aim of the project was to give London its first private gallery space big enough to take major exhibitions from New York or Los Angeles.

The ground floor of the old garages has been converted to provide three galleries, the largest being at the centre of the site. This 28- by 13-metre space has four big rooflights providing diffused lighting. The second space, 22 by 11 metres, is in a linear shed alongside the railway, while the smallest gallery occupies an old warehouse. All three have full environmental controls. The first floor, reached by a steel stair rising from the entrance gallery, accommodates offices and viewing rooms.

The thick walls enclosing the sequence of large gallery spaces have wide thresholds between them. The absence of skirtings or articulation gaps at their base gives a sense of permanence, and the services the walls contain are satisfactorily hidden. The concrete gallery floors have a lightly sand-blasted finish and can support heavy sculpture.

A loading bay, large enough to handle big artworks, has an ingenious door that, when closed, forms part of the gallery walls. When necessary, the whole wall can be temporarily removed. The quality of daylight, supplemented artificially only when required, is universally effective, providing an even light level on hanging zones. Detailing is inventive and simple and fits well with the purity of the spaces.

The office furniture, made of oak-faced blockboard with exposed and polished cores, is an inventive example of the level of detail design to be found throughout.

The architecture does not seek to upstage the art that it contains. But in complementing it, a strong architectural context has been created.

CLIENT GAGOSIAN GALLERY
STRUCTURAL ENGINEER PRICE & MYERS
SERVICES ENGINEER MAX FORDHAM LLP
QS JACKSON COLES
CONTRACTOR INTERIOR PLC
CONTRACT VALUE CONFIDENTIAL
DATE OF COMPLETION MAY 2004
GROSS INTERNAL AREA 1800 SQUARE METRES
PHOTOGRAPHER HÉLÈNE BINET

HOUSE AND STUDIO, DEPTFORD .LONDON SE8 .DSDHA

This is DSDHA's first one-off house, surprisingly perhaps, since houses are the projects on which so many young architects cut their teeth. The site is surrounded by a fragmented urban zone of empty plots, blank walls and the backs of buildings. Though determinedly modern, this is a house that acknowledges the history of the site and the area.

The building is, in effect, a semi-detached villa. But it comes with neither the large budget nor the preconceptions with which so many residential clients lumber inexperienced architects. Indeed, the low budget helped in determining a modesty of scale and materials, many of which were salvaged and recycled. These included bricks and granite setts, and some of the timbers, which were beachcombed by the client along the Thames foreshore.

Under a long monopitch roof and divided by a shared party wall, two simple uses abut. On one side, and planned around a small entrance courtyard, is a double-height workspace. On the other, similarly planned around the smallest of courtyards but entered under the tallest wall, is a simple dwelling. On the ground floor are a living space and a bathroom, and a stair leads to an upper bedroom under the high end of the monopitch: this looks out over the boundary wall to a small park. While its construction from second-hand bricks and galvanized windows and metalwork seems rugged and appropriately tough, the planning of the building with its open courtyards, while it engages openly with the adjacent street, does leave it disarmingly vulnerable.

In an area where it must have been tempting to turn one's back on the outside world, this building seeks to be part of the city in which it finds itself. It is carefully built, the detailing is uncompromising, and the choice of materials is restrained. It is an exemplary response to its urban setting.

CLIENT PRIVATE
STRUCTURAL ENGINEER PRICE & MYERS
CONTRACTOR EMERSON WILLIS LTD
CONTRACT VALUE £225,000
DATE OF COMPLETION JULY 2005
GROSS INTERNAL AREA 115 SQUARE METRES
PHOTOGRAPHER HÉLÈNE BINET

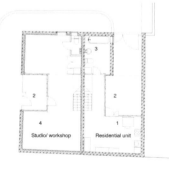

GROUND-FLOOR PLAN

Studio/ workshop   Residential unit

INSTITUTE OF CELL AND MOLECULAR SCIENCE, THE BLIZARD BUILDING .LONDON E1 .SMC ALSOP/AMEC DESIGN & MANAGEMENT

The Institute of Cell and Molecular Science is part of an attempt to create a world-class medical school. It brings together nearly four hundred scientists, previously inefficiently scattered across a number of sites, in one big building that is flexible enough to respond to the changing needs of a scientific community and open enough to engender collaboration, while affording privacy where needed. Scientists took part in workshops with the architects to help determine the nature of the building that would become their place of work. The glazed building is both transparent and reflective, metaphorically offering insights into academic scientific research while suggesting the analytical nature of the subject in question.

Four pods hanging in the glass pavilion house meeting rooms and an exhibition display space. The lower-ground-floor laboratories are zoned according to the nature of the research, and the more accessible of them can be seen from the central staircase. Those involved in more delicate scientific research are housed beneath the ground-floor offices. Research results are written up in the glazed offices on the upper floors.

The building is generous in terms of public space, with good circulation routes that are easy to navigate. The extensive plant is housed in a separate building, linked by a glass walkway at first-floor level, that also houses a beautiful elliptical four-hundred-seat lecture theatre in shades of green.

The institute does everything that is asked of it. It takes the traditional idea of a laboratory building and adds a layer of sparkle. This is 'science as theatre', with all the operational props on display: rows of laboratory coats and banks of sterilized jars lined up waiting for contents. Science has suddenly become glamorous – and interesting.

CLIENT QUEEN MARY UNIVERSITY OF LONDON
STRUCTURAL ENGINEER ADAMS KARA TAYLOR
SERVICES ENGINEER WSP
QS TURNER & TOWNSEND
CONTRACTOR LAING O'ROURKE
CONTRACT VALUE £34 MILLION
DATE OF COMPLETION MARCH 2005
GROSS INTERNAL AREA 9000 SQUARE METRES
PHOTOGRAPHER MORLEY VON STERNBERG

QUEEN MARY UNIVERSITY OF LONDON SHORTLISTED FOR THE RIBA/ARTS COUNCIL ENGLAND CLIENT OF THE YEAR

THE INSTITUTE OF CELL AND MOLECULAR SCIENCE WAS REVISITED BY THE RIBA AWARDS GROUP AND CONSIDERED FOR THE STIRLING SHORTLIST

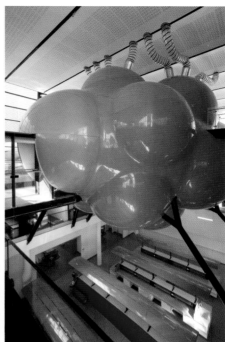

JOHN PERRY CHILDREN'S CENTRE AND NURSERY
.DAGENHAM .DSDHA

The two buildings that make up this project are the Nursery Centre (phase 1) and the Children's Centre (phase 2). The Nursery Centre has twenty-six places and the Children's Centre fifty places with daycare, all for local children. Additionally, as there is no hospital provision in the London Borough of Barking and Dagenham, the Children's Centre has paediatric facilities.

The headteacher of the nursery was determined to give children more in their lives than being ferried from home to school and back, experiencing little or nothing of a world they saw only on TV. The idea she developed with the architects was based on the Barbara Hepworth Studio: a studio for children where the fourth wall opens out on the inspiration of nature, in the shape of an existing courtyard that would provide a 'learning landscape'.

In the centre for older children the courtyard is placed at the heart of the building, bringing light to all its corners and acting as a walled garden for the children's play and enlightenment.

Both buildings are single storey and respond intelligently to the client's brief. From any approach, they stand proud in comparative scale. In addition, external mirrored artwork at child height provides stimulation and animation at the junction between the two centres and the schools.

The industrial brick façades of the buildings work well in the formal landscape and reflect the changing environment. The detailing includes an interior of cork cladding with a layer of timber that lines up well with the door heights. Mirrors and glazing above the internal walls introduce light into the centre of the building. Interior glazed walls offer visual connection to the front entrance without compromising security or privacy.

CLIENT CHILDREN'S SERVICES, LONDON BOROUGH OF BARKING AND DAGENHAM
STRUCTURAL ENGINEER PRICE & MYERS
SERVICES CONSULTANT PEARCE ASSOCIATES
QS STOCKDALE
CONTRACTORS FOREST GATE CONSTRUCTION (PHASE 1)/LAKEHOUSE CONTRACTS LTD (PHASE 2)
CONTRACT VALUE £495,000 (PHASE 1)/ £1.2 MILLION (PHASE 2)
DATE OF COMPLETION JANUARY 2004 (PHASE 1)/DECEMBER 2005 (PHASE 2)
GROSS INTERNAL AREA 665 SQUARE METRES
PHOTOGRAPHER HÉLÈNE BINET

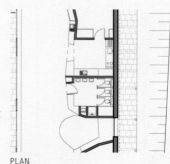

PLAN

LIGHT HOUSE
.LONDON W11 .GIANNI BOTSFORD ARCHITECTS

A big house has been squeezed into a back-land site in Notting Hill. It is entirely surrounded by other buildings and accessed through a small arch. Ingenuity has resolved all the challenges of providing privacy and light for a large family home encircled by neighbours.

It took a year to find a site in the area that could accommodate a house with five bedrooms, a suite of living rooms, a library, two studies, a wine cellar, a pool – and a chapel. What was found was a redundant warehouse with planning permission for change of use to a single dwelling. That, and the need for fourteen party-wall agreements, set the parameters for the design. Environmental engineers were commissioned to conduct a survey of the site in relation to its neighbours. This also greatly influenced the design in terms of optimizing daylight penetration. As a result the section was inverted – bedrooms on the ground floor, living spaces above – around a double-height piano nobile, and under a 'sky façade', an entirely glazed roof that uses different degrees of fritting to filter light to suit the functions of the rooms beneath.

The house is designed from the inside out in order to turn the site's disadvantages into benefits. In-situ exposed concrete provides the structural strength for ambitious spans, lends thermal mass to a naturally ventilated house and gives it its robust finish.

A vision that sets out to exploit the potential of the site in a modern, disciplined way has been relentlessly followed through over several years, and the detailed design is exquisite.

CLIENT PRIVATE
ENGINEER ARUP
LANDSCAPE ARCHITECT LUSZCZAC ASSOCIATES
QS TIM GATEHOUSE ASSOCIATES
CONTRACTOR DAY BUILDING LTD
CLIENT REPRESENTATIVE MALCOLM READING ASSOCIATES
PARTY-WALL SURVEYOR ROGER RAWLINSON ASSOCIATES
CONTRACT VALUE CONFIDENTIAL
DATE OF COMPLETION OCTOBER 2005
GROSS INTERNAL AREA 800 SQUARE METRES
PHOTOGRAPHER HÉLÈNE BINET

SHORTLISTED FOR THE MANSER MEDAL

FIRST FLOOR PLAN

LOCK-KEEPER'S GRADUATE CENTRE
.LONDON E1 .SURFACE ARCHITECTS

This delightful little folly is situated on the edge of the Grand Union Canal running through east London. It is attached to an early Victorian lock-keeper's cottage, until recently privately owned, on the Queen Mary University of London campus. When the owners decided to move on and sold the house, the university bought it with a view to development.

The building is now used as a graduate centre, with small lecture rooms and a chill-out/relaxation space. On the ground floor of the cottage are computer cluster rooms. The new building also enlarges the reception area that currently houses a display about the history of the lock-keeper's cottage. The connecting foyer is clad in strips of framed panelling finished with coloured renders and structural glazing.

The young practice has designed a contemporary steel-frame extension as a series of interlocking forms around the north and west sides of the old cottage. The dominant aluminium-clad north wing projects across the towpath and contains a common room with great views towards the lock. It is angled so that views of the cottage from the other side of the canal are not obscured.

The crazy geometry of the centre lends itself well to the small scale – it is only 249 square metres. But the colours of the building (grey externally, bright internally) and the sloping windows and odd angles draw attention to it.

The architects have exercised a degree of bravado with this tiny building, particularly in its relationship with the existing structure. Where would you find such a delightful boundary-pushing scheme but in the diverse eccentricity of London?

CLIENT QUEEN MARY UNIVERSITY OF LONDON
ENGINEER MITCHELL-HORTON
SERVICES ENGINEER TGA
CONTRACTOR CHARTER CONSTRUCTION PLC
QS AND PLANNING SUPERVISOR TRINNICK TURNER (NOW P.H. WARR)
CONTRACT VALUE £644,509
DATE OF COMPLETION MARCH 2005
GROSS INTERNAL AREA 249 SQUARE METRES
PHOTOGRAPHERS KILIAN O'SULLIVAN – VIEW/HUFTON + CROW – VIEW (LEFT)

SHORTLISTED FOR THE STEPHEN LAWRENCE PRIZE

QUEEN MARY UNIVERSITY OF LONDON SHORTLISTED FOR THE RIBA/ARTS COUNCIL ENGLAND CLIENT OF THE YEAR

GROUND-FLOOR PLAN

NATIONAL POLICE MEMORIAL
.LONDON SW1 .FOSTER AND PARTNERS

Cambridge Green, at the end of The Mall at Horse Guards Road, has for too long been a neglected public space. After considerable negotiation the site, dominated by a mysterious, Brutalist, windowless and ivy-covered MOD structure, and including a concrete vent shaft, was made available for the National Police Memorial. The construction of a new memorial could provide appropriate peace and dignity, and it could also resolve the problems of this nationally significant site.

A book of remembrance is contained in a window below the Metropolitan Police crest, which is inscribed into the black granite of one end of an enclosure that also envelopes the vent shaft. This front subtly projects proud of the sides against which ivy is now growing. Placed forward and to one side of this is a 7-metre-tall tower made from single sheets of annealed glass laid one on top of another. This tower stands in a rectangular pool and is lit at night from within and without by a dim blue light that touchingly recalls the traditional sign of safety and help used by police in past times.

The composition is extraordinarily simple. The whole, however, is substantially greater than the sum of its parts. While the group of refined architectural elements achieves a calm introspection appropriate to the task, the asymmetrical planning deliberately includes in its composition the rock-like structure of the government building that has stood for so long without apparent purpose. A new space has been made that is quite as restrained and dignified as the carefully considered elements that make it. And it succeeds as a memorial, in that it evokes a sense of mingled past and future, of sadness and pride.

CLIENTS NATIONAL POLICE MEMORIAL TRUST/MICHAEL WINNER
STRUCTURAL ENGINEER WATERMAN PARTNERSHIP
SERVICES CONSULTANT WATERMAN GORE
LANDSCAPE ARCHITECT CHARLES FUNCKE ASSOCIATES
QS DAVIS LANGDON LLP
CONTRACTOR BOVIS LEND LEASE
CONTRACT VALUE CONFIDENTIAL
DATE OF COMPLETION APRIL 2005
PHOTOGRAPHER NIGEL YOUNG

NEW CLASSROOMS AT HALLFIELD SCHOOL .LONDON W2 .CARUSO ST JOHN ARCHITECTS

Two new classroom blocks have been inserted into the original school designed by Drake and Lasdun as part of the Hallfield Estate, which was masterplanned by Berthold Lubetkin's practice Tecton between 1947 and 1950. The existing school is listed Grade II*. The original design was highly influential: clusters of single-storey infants' classrooms enclosed by two-storey accommodation for juniors providing an intimate, Arcadian atmosphere. It is considered by many – not just former pupils – to be their favourite school building.

The architects have successfully inserted new buildings into the plan without compromising its integrity. In fact they have greatly improved it by removing a disparate collection of Portakabins that had been used for teaching for the last quarter of a century. Furthermore, the design and choice of materials have involved a subtle reinterpretation of the original school, developed with an empathy that is neither too reverential nor too assertive. The new work, with the agreement of the client, is designed as a scheme complete in itself, and not to be extended further.

The client has clearly made the right choice in selecting architects of this calibre to reinterpret the original concept, and has supported them in implementing the scheme. Some of the detail design is ingenious, especially the simple ventilation arrangements that illustrate the tenacity the architects have shown in seeing through such important additions while addressing modern environmental requirements.

CLIENT WESTMINSTER CITY COUNCIL
STRUCTURAL ENGINEER PRICE & MYERS
SERVICES ENGINEER MAX FORDHAM LLP
QS M.H. JACKSON & ASSOCIATES
CONTRACTOR LAKEHOUSE CONTRACTS
CONTRACT VALUE £1.75 MILLION
DATE OF COMPLETION JULY 2005
GROSS INTERNAL AREA 1000 SQUARE METRES
PHOTOGRAPHER HÉLÈNE BINET

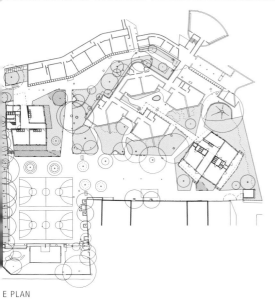

E PLAN

NEWINGTON GREEN STUDENT HOUSING
.LONDON N16 .HAWORTH TOMPKINS

The original Alliance Building of the China Inland Mission overlooking Newington Green has been restored and converted to hostel use. Surrounded by nineteenth-century housing stock, it forms a gateway to four new four- and five-storey hostel blocks on the landlocked site behind.

The client required two hundred student bed spaces arranged in apartments of five and seven en-suite study-bedrooms. Each apartment was to be provided with a self-contained kitchen/dining room. Construction was through a design-and-build contract with full design-team novation.

The four buildings have been arranged serially from the entrance, their position making good use of the mature trees and providing intimate spaces between them. The connecting path passes beneath the stairs and kitchen/ dining rooms of each building, threading together the more public areas of the scheme.

A strategy by which windows are arranged as a series of staggered vertical strips acts as an ingenious foil to the otherwise squat blocks, and gives buoyancy to each elevation. Timber windows, with their naturally finished metal sub-components, are part of a successful palette that includes an off-white render to external walls and unwrought sawn-timber screens to external staircases and galleries. The finishes and robust detailing are consistent throughout.

Internally, study-bedrooms have well-designed prefabricated showers and WCs. Each bedroom faces east or west and looks over the courtyard gardens. The tranquillity of the environment thus created is enjoyable and has been achieved at the modest cost of a little less than £1400 per square metre.

CLIENT SHAFTESBURY STUDENT HOUSING
STRUCTURAL ENGINEER R.J. WITT ASSOCIATES
SERVICES ENGINEERS BUILDING SERVICES SOLUTIONS AND ATELIER TEN
LANDSCAPE ARCHITECT COLVIN & MOGGRIDGE
QS GROVE & LAWRENCE
CONTRACTOR ROK LLEWELYN & SONS LTD
CONTRACT VALUE £7.68 MILLION
DATE OF COMPLETION AUGUST 2004
GROSS INTERNAL AREA 5324 SQUARE METRES
PHOTOGRAPHERS MORLEY VON STERNBERG (TOP)/PHILIP VILE

TYPICAL FLOOR PLAN

NILE STREET
.LONDON N1 .MUNKENBECK + MARSHALL
URBANISM

This housing project – keyworker studios, affordable-rental, shared-ownership and private flats – is place-making at its best. Interestingly, apart from the single stand-alone block of six private-sale flats at the west of the site the flat types are integrated within the two south and north blocks. The affordable-rental flats are indistinguishable from other tenures.

Street elevations are covered with green copper cladding interspersed with sustainable timber bands that wrap round the building. Most flats have generous external space in the form of balconies or terraces, many in the familiar Munkenbeck + Marshall triangular form. All of the flats have access to a roof terrace equipped with planters and benches. The central ground-floor courtyard of the scheme has a pool and rill (designed by Antony Donaldson) within formal hard landscaping and planting. Inside, the apartments have double-height spaces that make for good lighting.

The Egyptian theme suggested by the scheme's Nile Street address is expressed in the hieroglyphic symbols on the curved concierge windows and the stainless-steel windbreak panels on the roof terrace. Here in the centre of London, where more and more residents cycle to work, Nile Street's circular bike store softens the formal landscape. Extra facilities on site include a basement youth centre, hard-ball court and playground.

The architects have shown great skill in accommodating a high-density building on the site while retaining privacy for individual flats. They have also managed to promote a sense of community by the careful use of shared space.

CLIENT PEABODY TRUST
STRUCTURAL ENGINEER ELLIS AND MOORE
SERVICES ENGINEER ATELIER TEN
SCULPTOR ANTONY DONALDSON
QS E.C. HARRIS
CONTRACTOR MANSELL CITY
CONTRACT VALUE £17.3 MILLION
DATE OF COMPLETION DECEMBER 2005
GROSS INTERNAL AREA 11,450 SQUARE METRES
PHOTOGRAPHER MORLEY VON STERNBERG

TYPICAL FLOOR PLAN

PARLIAMENT HILL SCHOOL
.LONDON NW5 .HAVERSTOCK ASSOCIATES

The site of this new single-storey laboratory building lies between the original early twentieth-century school fronting Highgate Road and a four-storey 1960s classroom block to the rear. A range of small-scale accommodation connects these two buildings, creating a space enclosed on three sides.

The new building is slightly serpentine, to link the entrances to the two existing main buildings. It provides the fourth side of what has now become a grassed court, containing three design and technology laboratories. A covered way subtly undulates in response to both the plan and the changes of site levels. It is supported on slender steel props and provides a popular place for students to meet. The lightweight galvanized plated roof of the covered way contrasts with the green roof of the new building with its sedum planting. This in turn gives an agreeable continuity with the grassed area the new building now encloses. The main roof is punctuated, apparently at random, with cedar-clad rooflight turrets of varying heights. These give added interest and constitute a miniature roofscape, particularly when viewed from the upper storeys of the classroom block.

The laboratories receive their daylight screened through the rooflights. The high reveals of their interiors, painted yellow, give an illusion of sunlight and provide a contrast to the cooler, obscured glazing of the north elevation. South-facing rooms benefit from small window openings and the sun screening provided by the covered way.

The design has evolved with sustainability in mind. Internal temperatures are regulated by thermal mass, and this, together with heat recovery and the use of heat created by users, has resulted in a virtually self-heated building.

CLIENT LONDON BOROUGH OF CAMDEN
STRUCTURAL ENGINEER JENKINS & POTTER ENGINEERS
SERVICES ENGINEER CBG CONSULTANTS
LANDSCAPE CONSULTANT JOHN TIERNEY ASSOCIATES
QS NIGEL ROSE & PARTNERS
CONTRACTOR GEE CONSTRUCTION
CONTRACT VALUE £1.6 MILLION
DATE OF COMPLETION MAY 2005
GROSS INTERNAL AREA 500 SQUARE METRES
PHOTOGRAPHER DENNIS GILBERT – VIEW

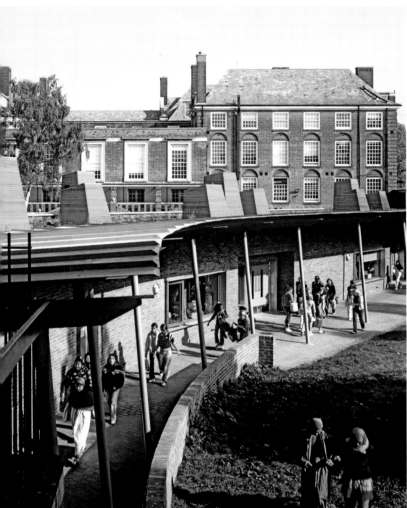

SITE PLAN

SIOBHAN DAVIES STUDIOS .LONDON SE1 .SARAH WIGGLESWORTH ARCHITECTS

This building has been a long time in the making. During the lengthy search for a site, an inventive dance company turned a theoretical conversation with an architect into a healthy and real collaboration. It was always likely that the site, with its two Victorian school buildings, neither large enough, facing an undistinguished street, would provoke a bold response. Such happy combinations of client, architect and site often lead the local regeneration of an area.

The occupation of the existing buildings is straightforward, robust and unsentimental. The rooms are stripped out and given new uses, and the area between the buildings becomes a galleried space leading to a new stair and core at the back of the building overlooking the existing school playground. Here, a 'sprung' stair takes dancers up to the smaller studio and changing rooms on the first floor and the new main studio on the second. A complex ribboned roof structure ballooning above the Victorian façade brings lots of daylight into the dance studio below.

The deliberately uneasy outcome of the relationship between new and old avoids the image of an institution fixed in time. The conclusion of this collaboration between architect and client looks as if it is ever ready to be added to or changed.

In line with the practice's green philosophy, this is a naturally ventilated building. Tempered fresh air is introduced by means of earth tubes, which mean the air is cool in summer and warm in winter. The user has control over the mechanical ventilation system.

The making of the building may sometimes seem haphazard, but the outcome, being far from precious, leaves plenty of room in which its occupants may think as well as dance.

CLIENT DANCERS' STUDIO TRUST
STRUCTURAL ENGINEER PRICE & MYERS
SERVICES ENGINEER FULCRUM CONSULTING
PROJECT MANAGER JACKSON COLES
ACOUSTIC DESIGN PAUL GILLIERON ACOUSTIC DESIGN
ACCESS ALL CLEAR DESIGN
THEATRE LIGHTING AND SOUND CHARCOALBLUE
QS BOYDEN & COMPANY
CONTRACTOR ROOFF LTD
CONTRACT VALUE £2.4 MILLION
DATE OF COMPLETION JANUARY 2006
GROSS INTERNAL AREA 770 SQUARE METRES
PHOTOGRAPHER RICHARD BRYANT – ARCAID

UCL SCHOOL OF SLAVONIC AND EAST EUROPEAN STUDIES
.LONDON WC1 .SHORT AND ASSOCIATES

The School of Slavonic and East European Studies is on a severely restricted site. The plan radiates symmetrically about the entrance. To the rear and over five floors a semicircular ring of academic offices encloses a stacked library. This enclosure is completed by a similar strip of offices facing the street but separated from it by a detached and arcaded brick façade. A central full-height lightwell provides visual connection to the entrance from all floors.

The façade, with its inner skin set some 1.5 metres back, accommodates two single-flight stairs that ascend from either side of the entrance and terminate at the first floor. From there, circulation continues to upper floors by conventional dogleg flights. The brick façade of this new building challenges the academic orthodoxy of glass elevations and sun screening. It also expresses the staircases. The relationship of the entrance to the central hall and from there to the library floors and offices provides surprisingly successful intimacy in a building of this size, encouraging interaction between departments.

The design has been underpinned by the principles of sustainability. Passive down-draught cooling relies on the reservoir of cool air in the central five-storey hall. Air is drawn in around its top and exhausted via high vertical stacks that contribute to the characteristic exterior expression. In winter, fresh air enters the central lightwell at low level and flows to upper floors after being warmed. In the summer, ambient air is cooled mechanically by chilled water flowing through coils at the head of the lightwell. The cooled air then fills the lightwell and ventilates the adjoining usable spaces.

The design, then, is concerned as much with energy conservation as it is with architectural history. The result is a green building that is engagingly idiosyncratic, and reminiscent of a small palazzo.

CLIENT UCL
STRUCTURAL ENGINEER MARTIN STOCKLEY ASSOCIATES
SERVICES ENGINEER ENVIRONMENTAL DESIGN PARTNERSHIP
LANDSCAPE ARCHITECT SLAINE CAMPBELL
QS AND PROJECT MANAGER TURNER TOWNSEND
SUSTAINABILITY CONSULTANT INSTITUTE OF ENERGY AND SUSTAINABLE DESIGN, DE MONTFORT UNIVERSITY
LIGHTING CONSULTANT SUTTON VANE ASSOCIATES
SPECIALIST LIGHTING DESIGN LAMPS AND CANDLES
TYPOGRAPHER INCISIVE LETTERWORK
CONTRACTOR WILLMOTT DIXON
CONTRACT VALUE £10.05 MILLION
DATE OF COMPLETION OCTOBER 2005
GROSS INTERNAL AREA 3800 SQUARE METRES
PHOTOGRAPHER PETER COOK – VIEW

SHORTLISTED FOR THE RIBA SUSTAINABILITY AWARD

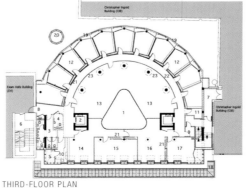

THIRD-FLOOR PLAN

UNICORN THEATRE
.LONDON SE1 .KEITH WILLIAMS ARCHITECTS

The Unicorn Theatre was founded soon after World War II as a peripatetic and innovative children's company, touring shows in two ex-MOD lorries. At last it has realized founder Caryl Jenner's dream of having a permanent base, and in the process it has become an innovative client. The artistic director, Tony Graham, was determined to have a grown-up building for children, one that did not patronize them in the way so many colourful, blobby buildings do.

As part of the 'More London' commercial development there was inevitable pressure to maximize the area of land available for profitable exploitation and to minimize the area on which the theatre could stand. This constraint has produced a design that had to be as carefully and intricately considered in cross-section as any theatre would be in plan. The solution to the problem is a bold cultural signal in a previously arid urban landscape.

The main theatre is planned at a raised level above the smaller workshop theatre, service bay and glass-fronted entrance foyer, which faces the corner of Tooley Street and the coincidentally named Unicorn Passage. The vertical organization of public facilities is carefully matched at each level by well-planned back-of-house accommodation. The surprisingly generous amount of internal space over a number of levels is elegantly disguised by the restrained representation of the external volumes.

This building puts the Unicorn Theatre firmly on the map with much-needed and well-resolved new facilities. During the day the external architectural representation is powerful in its volume but polite in its detail. At night the interior connects dramatically with the outside world, making Tooley Street a place to go to rather than simply to pass by.

CLIENT UNICORN CHILDREN'S CENTRE
STRUCTURAL ENGINEER ARUP
SERVICES CONSULTANT ARUP
ACOUSTICIAN ARUP ACOUSTICS
QS BUCKNALL AUSTIN
CONTRACTOR MANSELL CONSTRUCTION SERVICES
CONTRACT VALUE £9.25 MILLION
DATE OF COMPLETION NOVEMBER 2006
GROSS INTERNAL AREA 3640 SQUARE METRES
PHOTOGRAPHER HÉLÈNE BINET

UNICORN THEATRE WAS REVISITED BY THE RIBA AWARDS GROUP AND CONSIDERED FOR THE STIRLING SHORTLIST

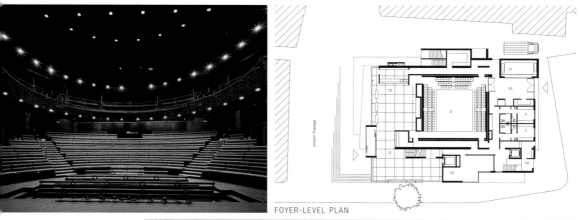

FOYER-LEVEL PLAN

KILEN
.FREDERIKSBERG, DENMARK .LUNDGAARD & TRANBERG ARCHITEKTFIRMA

'Kilen' means wedge in Danish; a four-storey wedge-shaped building sits on top of an organically shaped one-storey base and forms a new home for a business-studies faculty. It is built on former railway lands, above the new metro that links all the buildings on Copenhagen Business School's campus.

Open communal and lecture theatres on the ground floor are combined with a range of smaller meeting and teaching rooms on the upper four floors. The internal spaces are linked, visually and practically, by a generous atrium that reaches up through the full height of the building.

The ethos of the faculty is based on self-motivation and learning through communication. The building embodies this approach in its generous circulation routes and informal meeting spaces; it also avoids closed, cellular rooms. Teaching and meeting spaces that do have to be enclosed mainly use glazed screens between them and the generous circulation spaces.

The exterior of the building is fully glazed but screened by elegant adjustable panels that control solar gain and add visual interest through a combination of materials including metal, glass and wood. The pale, muted-coloured panels give it the look almost of a Sauerbruch Hutton scheme bleached by the sun. The screening makes the offices comfortable places to work even in the heat of the short Danish summer and also creates attractive views out by managing glare. The appearance of the building shifts with the time of day, the changing seasons and the uses to which the rooms behind the variously angled shutters are being put.

A limited palette of materials has been so skilfully deployed that the result is outstanding.

CLIENT COPENHAGEN BUSINESS SCHOOL
ENGINEER NIRAS A/S
CONTRACTOR E. PIHL & SON A/S
CONTRACT VALUE 191 MILLION DANISH KRONE
DATE OF COMPLETION DECEMBER 2005
GROSS INTERNAL AREA 13,100 SQUARE METRES
PHOTOGRAPHER JENS LINDHE

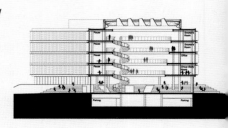

SECTION THROUGH ATRIUM

FEDERAL ENVIRONMENTAL AGENCY
.DESSAU, GERMANY .SAUERBRUCH HUTTON
ARCHITECTS

Built for the German government's environmental agency as a showcase for its work, on heavily polluted land in an area of Dessau that still looks desperately abandoned, this project has an almost surreal polish. It stands like a vivid advertisement for the new Germany amid the all-too-evident remains of the old. But this is far more than a brightly coloured architectural bauble; it is extremely well controlled and its consistent detailing and the excellence of its construction lend homogeneity to a very large office building.

Arrival is via the Forum, a crescent-shaped glazed-in public area that gives access to information and to a self-contained and windowless concert hall. The central atrium is a calm and quiet place, enlivened by coloured glass panels applied to the outside of the timber-framed windows. The fuzzy transparency of the panels creates varying degrees of opacity as you move up the building, a glamorous counterpoint to the natural materials used in the atrium and around the snaking exterior envelope. Circulation is very generous, with long central corridors connecting the cellular offices and the atrium serving as an alternative way of moving between departments.

Two other freestanding buildings complete the campus: an elegantly glazed pavilion houses the café, and a library somewhat bizarrely incorporates the red-brick booking hall of an old railway station that used to occupy the site.

The other surprise for visitors from the UK is to see that all the office spaces are cellular; that is still the German way, although the architects pushed the clients as hard as they could. The clients are very pleased with the building and are keen to stress that this project is of national as well as local significance.

CLIENT FEDERAL ENVIRONMENTAL AGENCY
STRUCTURAL ENGINEER KREBS UND KIEFER
ENERGY CONSULTANT ZIBELL WILLNER & PARTNER
LANDSCAPE CONSULTANT ST RAUM A
QS HARMS & PARTNER
CONTRACTOR HOCHTIEF CONSTRUCTION AG
CONTRACT VALUE € 42.5 MILLION
DATE OF COMPLETION MAY 2005
GROSS INTERNAL AREA 39,800 SQUARE METRES
PHOTOGRAPHERS JAN BITTER/ANNETTE KISLING (RIGHT)

THE FEDERAL ENVIRONMENT AGENCY WAS VISITED BY THE RIBA AWARDS GROUP AND CONSIDERED FOR THE STIRLING SHORTLIST

GROUND-FLOOR PLAN

183 .EUROPEAN

THE FRIEDER BURDA COLLECTION MUSEUM .BADEN BADEN, GERMANY .RICHARD MEIER & PARTNERS

This new gallery shows that a modern pavilion need not be incompatible with an eighteenth-century park setting. It is a pleasant surprise to come across this lovely little building – all glass and gleaming white aluminium – in the magnificent Lichtentaler Allee Park, the green heart of the spa town of Baden Baden. The scale of the new museum is equivalent to that of the neighbouring nineteenth-century Neo-classical buildings that house grand hotels and spa-baths, as well as the Kunsthalle, the art gallery next door, to which the Meier building is linked by a somewhat over-assertive bridge.

The interior is a triumph. The framed views of the parkland add drama to the gallery experience. The architectural promenade proceeding from the entrance lobby via the ramp to the various galleries forms the essential armature. In this highly controlled white universe one can imagine the Abstract Expressionists or the accident paintings of Andy Warhol being particularly at home. Great care has been taken to minimize extraneous secondary detail such as grilles and switches. The design of the interior of the lift, which is shared by visitors and art, is particularly successful. Heating, cooling, structure, fire escape and wayfinding, so frequently unnecessary distractions to the gallery-going public, are well under control.

When Meier used this architectural language in his private houses on Long Island in the 1970s the results could be considered over-rhetorical in a domestic context, but here it is perfectly appropriate in a public building of great quality.

CLIENT STIFTUNG FRIEDER BURDA
ASSOCIATE ARCHITECT PETER W. KRUSE
STRUCTURAL ENGINEER SCHUMER & KIENZLE
LANDSCAPE ARCHITECT BERND WEIGEL
CONTRACT VALUE CONFIDENTIAL
DATE OF COMPLETION 2004
GROSS INTERNAL AREA 2000 SQUARE METRES
PHOTOGRAPHER ROLAND HALBE

ÁRAS CHILL DARA, DEVOY PARK .NAAS, IRELAND .HENEGHAN.PENG ARCHITECTS WITH ARTHUR GIBNEY & PARTNERS

One of the great successes of the reorganization of local government in Ireland is the proliferation of good town halls springing up in regional centres; the RIBA has recently rewarded Fingal, Limerick, Carlow and Athlone. Taken together, they represent a level of optimism and confidence in public procurement that the UK cannot begin to match. A feature of these commissions, often won in open competition, is that they have launched the careers of several young architects.

Heneghan.Peng are masters of the competition win; since winning this one while based in New York, they have landed The Grand Museum of Egypt and the Giant's Causeway Visitor Centre. To deliver the job, they teamed up with the Dublin practice of Arthur Gibney & Partners, one of the best of an older generation of Irish architects.

This local authority services centre is built on a sloping lawn facing the street on the site of an old barracks. The brief was for a building that would seem open, democratic and accessible. The lawn tilts it towards the street and a single footpath leads into an open court addressing the main public space. Informal glass and metal lean-tos provide shade and form cloister-like passageways around the sides of the court. Here a footpath leads directly into an interior dominated by a switchback ramp that takes you floor by floor through all the council's services.

For a first building, this project has been developed with singular confidence and brio. While it is a credit to the singular vision of the architects, both the client and the Royal Institute of the Architects of Ireland must take a considerable share of the praise for having the confidence to commission untried architects to carry out such significant work. This is, after all, in the grand tradition of Thomas Cooley and Paul Koralek.

CLIENTS KILDARE COUNTY COUNCIL/ NAAS TOWN COUNCIL
CIVIL AND STRUCTURAL ENGINEER MICHAEL PUNCH & PARTNERS
SERVICES ENGINEER BURO HAPPOLD
FAÇADE/RAMP ENGINEER RFR
LIGHTING ENGINEER BARTENBACH LICHTLABOR GMBH
QS BOYD CREED SWEETT
CONTRACTOR PIERSE CONTRACTING
CONTRACT VALUE € 42 MILLION
DATE OF COMPLETION JANUARY 2006
GROSS INTERNAL AREA 11,300 SQUARE METRES
PHOTOGRAPHER HISAO SUZUKI

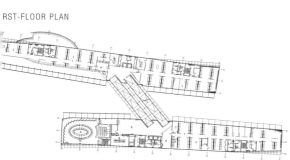

87 .EUROPEAN

POUSTINIA
.KILSHEELAN, IRELAND .ARCHITECTS BATES MAHER

'Poustinia' is a Russian word denoting a small cabin set aside for silence and prayer. This remarkable project is for three such buildings set in the grounds of a Rosminian house of prayer in the Comeragh Mountains in south-east Ireland. They are cut into a steep hillside, cantilevering over a wildflower meadow and the valley beyond. The window from the double bedroom of each cabin carefully frames the best views of the hill opposite. A fourth poustinia, by contrast, is built at the foot of the hill, next to the big house and hard against a stream, the sound and sight of which are evident throughout.

The faceted exteriors of the poustinias are clad with larch and fir battens, and a huge full-height section of the wall pivots to give entry. Each cabin is wrapped around a tiny internal courtyard paved with rough limestone rubble, which provides a meditative and contemplative heart. These tight wedges narrow towards the outside, taking the form of a vertical slot that allows the landscape subliminally to penetrate the cabin.

The interiors, though minimally detailed, are surprisingly rich in feel. Bathrooms are lined with varnished boarding, giving them the feeling of ablution facilities on a well-appointed yacht. Kitchen/living rooms flow into the bedroom (more of a wide corridor, really, leading to the bathroom – although the big views don't make it feel like that). Bespoke furniture made from lustrous dark hardwood is used throughout. It is no wonder that the poustinias have proved very popular with people seeking to recuperate from the pressures of contemporary existence, or searching for a new direction in their lives.

CLIENT ROSMINIAN ORDER
ENGINEER GEOGHEAGAN CONSULTING
CONTRACTOR KIERAN DORAN
CONTRACT VALUE € 500,000
DATE OF COMPLETION MAY 2005
GROSS INTERNAL AREA 160 SQUARE METRES (FOUR 40-SQUARE-METRE CABINS)
PHOTOGRAPHER ROS KAVANAGH

ELEVATION AND
SITE PLAN

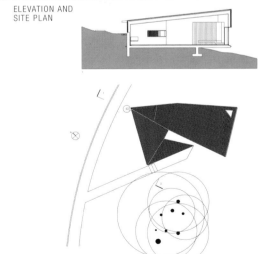

CAIXA GALICIA ART GALLERY
.LA CORUÑA, SPAIN .GRIMSHAW

The Caixa Galicia Art Gallery is lavishly funded by a 25 per cent levy imposed by government on financial institutions. This far-sighted policy has resulted in a permanent home for the Fundación Caixa Galicia's art collection, with sumptuous offices and a civic building that draws the public realm inside.

The building has temporary exhibition space and an auditorium on the lower ground floors, and an internet café and art bookshop at street level. Four permanent galleries occupy the upper floors, and the director's suite is located on the fifth and sixth floors.

The building's dramatic glazed façade is tilted forwards, with the ground cut away at street level, allowing light to flood into the four subterranean floors, which include a concert hall whose inspiration is clearly London's Royal Festival Hall. The skilful detailing to this façade has all the hallmarks of a Grimshaw design. The gallery spaces are clad in glass panels with a thin marble interlayer, while the atrium is clad in clear glass, allowing glimpses in from the street and out from the building. An inclined glass lift at one end offers the best free ride in town as it shoots precariously up the outside of the building. A suspended glazed screen on the street frontage allows backlit projections in the evening, making the building a focus for civic events from the entire harbour it sits within. This is clever rather than tricksy.

The character changes internally as a much more calmly detailed series of spaces emerges. The central atrium provides a welcoming but dramatic public room, and also acts as a public thoroughfare with a sculptural main staircase and a fire stair wrapping around one another, leading via glazed bridges to a series of individualized galleries.

CLIENT CAIXA CALICIA
STRUCTURAL AND SERVICES ENGINEER ARUP
QS DAVIS LANGDON EDETCO
CONTRACTOR DRAGADOS SA
CONTRACT VALUE CONFIDENTIAL
DATE OF COMPLETION FEBRUARY 2006
GROSS INTERNAL AREA 7693 SQUARE METRES
PHOTOGRAPHER EDMUND SUMNER – VIEW

CAIXA GALICIA ART GALLERY WAS VISITED BY THE RIBA AWARDS GROUP AND CONSIDERED FOR THE STIRLING SHORTLIST

SECTION

'A BRIDGE TOO FAR'
.MAOSI VILLAGE, GANSU, CHINA .PROFESSOR
EDWARD NG, CHINESE UNIVERSITY OF HONG KONG

Maosi Village is bisected by a branch of the Yellow River, across which villagers have traditionally waded to carry out their daily business. A series of wood and mud bridges intended to make life easier were regularly washed away by floods in the rainy season, meaning students were unable to attend school and, more seriously, claiming lives. The solution, devised by students working with design and construction professionals, was a bridge that rests on the riverbed and is designed to be submerged for 5 per cent of the year, standing 1.5 metres above the water for the rest of the time. In other words, it works with nature instead of fighting it.

The typical 'architectural' bridge is one that solves the problem of span, context and load in as elegant a manner as possible – with elegance defined as a certain leanness and the display of structural forces. 'A Bridge too Far' almost reverses this paradigm; it is modest and chunky but nonetheless brilliantly answers the demands of the context, which is here shaped mainly by social and economic forces.

The bridge had to be built to an extremely limited budget with unskilled labour using mainly local materials. The structural solution has a lovely logic to it without resorting to formalist pyrotechnics. Piers of gabion cages filled with local rock support a series of staggered sections – the stagger stabilizing and equalizing the loads as well as allowing individual sections to be lifted by a few people to clear any debris that might accumulate.

But the real delight is the choreography that this solution sets up: crossing the bridge becomes an event in its own right. Furthermore, the left-over space at each zigzag becomes a place to sit, so the bridge also becomes a social condenser. In all this, 'A Bridge too Far' goes way beyond being a thing that just joins two sides with a technical solution. It is a wonderful example of how inventive architectural and design thinking results in something both delightful and socially empowering.

CLIENT MAOSI VILLAGE GOVERNMENT
PROJECT PATRONS AND ADVISORS SIR DAVID AKERS-JONES, PETER WONG
DESIGN MANAGEMENT AND TEAM POLLY TSANG, KEVIN LI, LUCIA CHEUNG, PUI-MING CHAN, KAREN KIANG, MU JUN, JUH-KUEN HO, RYAN CHEUNG
STRUCTURAL ENGINEERS ANTHONY HUNT, RONAN COLLINS, PAUL TSANG, ANDREW LUONG, STEPHEN CHOW, PROFESSOR MOE CHEUNG
CONSTRUCTED BY VOLUNTEERS FROM THE CHINESE UNIVERSITY OF HONG KONG, HONG KONG PROFESSIONAL GREEN BUILDING COUNCIL, HONG KONG POLYTECHNICS UNIVERSITY, HONG KONG UNIVERSITY OF SCIENCE AND TECHNOLOGY, XIAN JAIOTONG UNIVERSITY, VILLAGERS OF MAOSI VILLAGE
CONTRACT VALUE £35,000
PHOTOGRAPHER EDWARD NG

THE WOHL CENTRE, BAR-ILAN UNIVERSITY .RAMAT-GAN, ISRAEL .STUDIO DANIEL LIBESKIND WITH THE HEDER PARTNERSHIP

The Wohl Centre – part of a new $500 million, 68-acre extension located to the north-east of Bar-Ilan University's central campus in Ramat-Gan – is the first building in Israel to be designed by Daniel Libeskind. The 3600-square-metre structure encompasses a nine-hundred-seat main auditorium – the largest on the university campus – three large lecture halls, and a multi-purpose foyer, providing space for performances, lectures, special events and conferences. Funded by the property developer Maurice Wohl, it is intended for use equally by the people of the town and the student population. The Heder Partnership, the Tel-Aviv-based architectural and interior design firm, served as associate architects.

The building stands at a crossroads on the university campus, acting as a beacon to the public and a gateway for the students, teachers and guests. It works equally well by day or night. The stone and metal exterior is homogeneous in form and penetrated by the slash windows first used by Libeskind at the Jewish Museum in Berlin.

Visitors enter a gracious lobby. This is the spatial heart of the building and acts as a dining and reception area for public functions. It can be subdivided into two separate areas, each of which can be joined up with adjacent seminar rooms. The auditorium is sculpted in the form of an open book, the steep sides of which add intimacy to the experience of giving or listening to a lecture or a performance. The auditorium can also be reconfigured in a number of ways to accommodate different audience sizes and numbers of simultaneous events.

This is another bravura performance from Libeskind, bringing scale, humanity and a feeling of new possibilities to an otherwise workaday university campus. Clearly built to a tight budget, the building makes a virtue of stark surfaces and uncluttered interiors, and a simple programme is imbued with enigma and a sense of the numinous.

CLIENT BAR-ILAN UNIVERSITY
STRUCTURAL ENGINEER J. KAHAN & PARTNERS STRUCTURE
LANDSCAPE ARCHITECT BAR-ILAN UNIVERSITY
CONTRACTOR OTRAM-SAHAR LTD
CONTRACT VALUE $9.6 MILLION
GROSS INTERNAL AREA 3900 SQUARE METRES
PHOTOGRAPHER BITTER BREDT

BRITISH COUNCIL
.LAGOS, NIGERIA .ALLIES AND MORRISON

The new British Council headquarters in Lagos is located in a high-security compound. Despite the constraints of this location, the client – the United Kingdom's international agency for cultural relations – needed a building that conveyed, above all, openness, transparency and accessibility.

One tenet of the British Council's architectural remit is that its overseas offices should reflect the values of the organization and project a contemporary image of the UK. The organization has an overseas property portfolio of some three hundred buildings, with a rolling programme of new works every year. The British Council believes that it should give new, young practices the opportunity to work on projects, enabling them to earn a higher profile in the international arena. Many have gone on to get commissions from other clients in that country.

The modest but assured design for the Lagos office is a well-judged response to existing white, rendered structures in the compound. A series of screens both protect the building and invite the visitor in: the first is a row of steel uprights cast in a low concrete wall forming the boundary of the site; the second is a screen of wood that shades the building; and the third is a curtain-wall system of bronze and glazing within.

The material palette of white rendering, exposed concrete and locally sourced Iroko timber, combined with the majestic height of the façade, helps to evoke both vernacular informality and the authority proper to a quasi-diplomatic institution. A wide-open ground floor of polished concrete constitutes the learning centre and leads to a café and garden in the rear. The British Council's local director occupies a glazed box above the reception desk on the upper-floor office level, visible to all in her not-so-private office.

CLIENT BRITISH COUNCIL
EXECUTIVE ARCHITECT JAMES CUBITT ARCHITECTS
STRUCTURAL ENGINEER ARUP
SERVICES ENGINEER KUNLE OGUNBAYO AND ASSOCIATES
QS AND PROJECT MANAGER TILLYARD
CONTRACT VALUE £800,000
GROSS INTERNAL AREA 750 SQUARE METRES
PHOTOGRAPHER DAVID GRABDORGE

KASTELLET SCHOOL
.OSLO, NORWAY .DIV.A ARKITEKTER

A school for six- to fifteen-year-olds with primary and secondary teaching for 560 pupils, this is about a third of the size of a typical British equivalent. It also incorporates a special-needs unit for multi-handicapped children, and these facilities are carefully integrated into the heart of the school.

Three wings containing the primary, middle and secondary schools are connected, through a series of bridges over the school street, to the communal facilities that house the assembly hall/gym, science and art rooms, library and administrative areas. There is much invention in the plan, most notably in the T-shaped classrooms that share large external learning terraces. Teaching is carried out in a variety of spaces, from large lecture rooms to smaller seminar spaces, and the building effortlessly encourages learning through its flexibility. Most innovatively, the home-economics area doubles up as the school café, a clever interpretation of the traditional brief.

Externally, the buildings are elegantly detailed using a combination of timber fins, steel and render. All teaching spaces have direct access to an undulating timber-decked landscape, the playful and sculptural nature of which acts as a backdrop for both learning and playing.

All Norwegian public buildings have to include works of art: in this case Antony Gormley was commissioned to make a piece called 'The Perpetual Pupil' that hangs below one of the bridges at the centre of the street.

The secret of Kastellet School is that it does not try too hard. Its minimal plan deals effortlessly with the complex nature of its brief while providing spaces that have character and flexibility. In Britain we are embarking on the biggest school-construction programme ever, and making some good buildings. However, this quiet and elegant school shows that we still have much to learn from our European colleagues.

CLIENT KASTELLET SCHOOL
STRUCTURAL ENGINEER STROMORKEN & HAMRE AS
SERVICES ENGINEER D.H. JØRGENSEN AS
INTERIOR ARCHITECT BEATE ELLINGSEN AS
QS BYGGANALYSE AS
ELECTRICAL ENGINEER STØLTUN AS
CONTRACTOR LID ENTREPRENOR AS
LANDSCAPE ØSTENGEN & BERGO AS
CONTRACT VALUE £15.6 MILLION
GROSS INTERNAL AREA 6700 SQUARE METRES
PHOTOGRAPHER JIRI HAUVEN

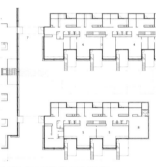

PART GROUND-FLOOR PLAN

DULNYOUK PUBLISHERS .PAJU BOOK CITY, SOUTH KOREA .FOREIGN OFFICE ARCHITECTS

This relatively small self-contained office building is ingenious in the way it carries a narrative about the site through into the organization and detail of the fabric. The long, narrow plan of the three-storey building, dictated by the masterplan, divides the suburban site between car park and garden, and continues the hard or soft language of external spaces into the interior on alternate floors. The hard elements facing the car park are therefore left as exposed concrete, while the interiors of the garden-facing elements are lined with merbau timber panelling.

The success of the project lies not only in the clear diagram that brings landscape into the building but also in the clarity with which spaces and structure have been organized. The exterior of the building is also intriguing, revealing the split personality of the diagram through the contrast of the timber-faced garden façade with the concrete façade facing the car park.

The quality of detailing underpins the bold concept, and the interior spaces are light, elegant and beautifully finished.

CLIENT DULNYOUK PUBLISHERS
ASSOCIATE ARCHITECT ALT STRUCTURAL ENGINEERING GROUP
LANDSCAPE DESIGN Y02 ARCHITECTS
CONTRACTOR DONGNKONG CONSTRUCTION
CONTRACT VALUE £1.8 MILLION
GROSS INTERNAL AREA 1800 SQUARE METRES
PHOTOGRAPHER KIM JAE-KYUNG

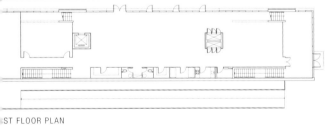

ST FLOOR PLAN

ZURICH AIRPORT
.ZURICH, SWITZERLAND .GRIMSHAW

The Airside and Landside Centres at Zurich Airport are the outcome of a 1996 competition. Physically unconnected, they contrast in terms of location, programme, vision and execution, yet they also display common themes.

The Airside Centre is essentially a two-level transit and waiting area in front of an array of existing buildings. It presents the public face of the airport both externally as a 'window' on the world of travel, in the form of a 250-metre-long glazed façade, and internally as a conduit for passengers. The architectural response is essentially a single gesture: a glorious space, lofty, open and light-filled with views out to the runways and the landscape beyond by day, and in to the relentless ebb and flow of passengers by night.

The dynamic sweeping concept for the building – evident in plan, section and elevation – achieved by a single wing form spread elegantly above the accommodation, is reinforced by the visible longitudinal lattice roof structure, the supporting steel 'A' frames and the continuous inclined glazed façade. The interior adheres to the concept while accommodating the conflicting requirements of unimpeded movement for some travellers and the desire to dawdle for other users of the space. The view out dominates: in the background is the shopping, with the retail outlets articulated as islands distributed throughout the hall like pieces of furniture.

In contrast, the Landside Centre has no external identity. Located above the train station, it is the link between the city's major public and private transport systems and the airport itself. The complex multi-layered intersections of entry and exit points are again unified and rationalized by space and light. This time, space has been carved through three deep levels, while natural light pours in through a vast elliptical rooflight overhead. Freestanding escalators connect check-in with retail and airport facilities via generous glazed circulation galleries.

The two centres comprise a bold intervention in which all is on display, each detail rigorously worked through, celebrated and consistently executed.

CLIENT UNIQUE (FLUGHAFEN ZURICH AG)
STRUCTURAL AND SERVICES ENGINEERS ERNST BASLER & PARTNERS/ARUP
QS PEROLINI BAUMANAGEMENT
CONTRACTOR UNIQUE (FLUGHAFEN ZURICH AG)
CONTRACT VALUE 600 MILLION SWISS FRANCS
GROSS INTERNAL AREA 800,000 SQUARE METRES
PHOTOGRAPHERW RALPH BENSBERG/ EDMUND SUMNER – VIEW (BOTTOM LEFT AND RIGHT)

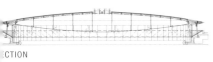

SECTION

173–176 PERRY STREET
.NEW YORK, USA .RICHARD MEIER & PARTNERS

A timely rebuke to almost all recent riverside residential development in London, these residential towers stand on either side of Perry Street in Greenwich Village, looking out confidently across the Hudson River, with unobstructed panoramic views of Manhattan and the New Jersey riverfront. The buildings are close to the newly renovated Hudson River Park, a network of green and paved open spaces providing a promenade for walkers, joggers, cyclists and rollerbladers all the way from Battery Park City to 59th Street.

The towers are Richard Meier's first construction in Manhattan. Their reductive elegance and stylistic understatement have given luxury urban living a new benchmark. The buildings are clad in insulating laminated glass and white metal panels with shadowboxes at the curtain wall expressing the individual floorplates. Their transparent minimal form is a striking addition to the New York City skyline.

The plan gets very close to an ideal of tower living – a combination of Le Corbusier's Domino frame and Mies van der Rohe's Farnsworth House stacked on fifteen floors, fully glazed on three sides of the extensive rectangular plan (approximately 21 by 15 metres). The fourth side is occupied by a bustle of two lifts and two escape stairs serving one apartment on each floor, maximizing the striking river views, which are enhanced by an expansive floor-to-ceiling glass curtain wall.

The domestic functions are generously and simply organized around a central core of bathrooms, with panoramic views around the perimeter. One might quibble about entering through the breakfast room and having to negotiate the ample freestanding circular columns, but this has not deterred some of Manhattan's most celebrated artistic residents from engaging in intense competition to occupy the higher floors.

CLIENT WEST PERRY, LLC
STRUCTURAL ENGINEER ROBERT SILMAN & ASSOCIATES
CONTRACTOR GOTHAM CONSTRUCTION CORPORATION
CONTRACT VALUE CONFIDENTIAL
GROSS INTERNAL AREA 36,620 SQUARE METRES
PHOTOGRAPHER SCOTT FRANCES

TWO-BEDROOM PLAN

MAPS, LISTS AND SPONSORS

SCOTLAND

2

1 3

NORTH

ULSTER

4, 5

NORTH-WEST

10 11 9

YORKSHIRE

7
6 8

15

17

EAST MIDLANDS

14

WALES WEST MIDLANDS

16

19

18

EAST

13

12

27

28

29

24 26

22

23

SOUTH

WESSEX

25

31

30

32

SOUTH-EAST

LONDON, SEE
PAGES 210–211

SOUTH-WEST

20 21

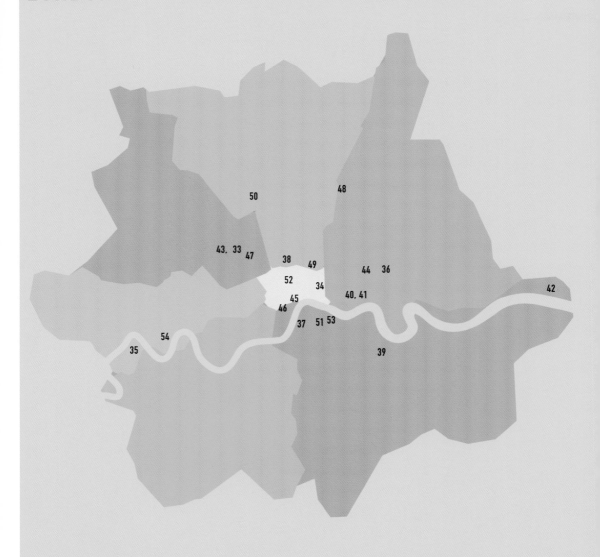

43. 33
47
50
48
38
49
52
34
45
46
44 36
40, 41
42
37 51 53
54
35
39

PREVIOUS WINNERS

THE STIRLING PRIZE

1996   Hodder Associates, University of Salford

1997   Michael Wilford & Partners, Music School, Stuttgart

1998   Foster and Partners, American Air Museum, Duxford

1999   Future Systems, NatWest Media Centre, Lord's, London

2000   Alsop & Störmer, Peckham Library, London

2001   Wilkinson Eyre Architects, Magna, Rotherham

2002   Wilkinson Eyre Architects, Millennium Bridge, Gateshead

2003   Herzog & De Meuron, Laban, London

2004   Foster and Partners, 30 St Mary Axe, London

2005   EMBT/RMJM, The Scottish Parliament, Edinburgh

THE ARCHITECTS' JOURNAL FIRST BUILDING AWARD

2001   Walker Architecture, Cedar House, Logiealmond

2002   Sutherland Hussey, Barnhouse, London

2003   De Rijke Marsh Morgan, No. 1 Centaur Street, London

2004   Annalie Riches, Silvia Ullmayer and Barti Garibaldo, In-Between, London

2005   Amin Taha Architects, Gazzano House, London

THE CROWN ESTATE CONSERVATION AWARD

1998   Peter Inskip and Peter Jenkins, Temple of Concord and Victory, Stowe

1999   Foster and Partners, the Reichstag, Berlin

2000   Foster and Partners, JC Decaux UK Headquarters, London

2001   Rick Mather Architects, Dulwich Picture Gallery, London

2002   Richard Murphy Architects with Simpson Brown Architects, Stirling Tolbooth

2003   LDN Architects, Newhailes House Conservation, Musselburgh

2004   HOK International, the King's Library, The British Museum, London

2005   Avanti Architects, Isokon (Lawn Road) Apartments, London

THE MANSER MEDAL

2001   Cezary Bednarski, Merthyr Terrace, London

2003   Burd, Haward, Marston Architects, Brooke Coombes House, London

2003   Jamie Fobert Architects, Anderson House, London

2004   Mole Architects, The Black House, Prickwillow

2005   Robert Dye Associates, Stealth House, London

THE RIBA CLIENT OF THE YEAR

1998   Roland Paoletti

1999   The MCC

2000   The Foreign and Commonwealth Office

2001   Molendinar Park Housing Association, Glasgow

2002   Urban Splash

2003   City of Manchester

2004   The Peabody Trust

2005   Gateshead Council

THE ADAPT TRUST ACCESS AWARD

2001   Avery Associates Architects, Royal Academy of Dramatic Arts, London

2002   Malcolm Fraser Architects, Dance Base,
Edinburgh

2003   Nicholl Russell Studios, The Space, Dundee
College

2003   Gumuchdjian Architects, Think Tank, Skibberreen,
Ireland

2004   Simon Conder Associates, Vista, Dungeness

2005   Niall McLaughlin Architects, House at Clonakilty

THE RIBA INCLUSIVE DESIGN AWARD

2004   Arup Associates, City of Manchester
Stadium

2005   Foster and Partners, The Sage Gateshead

THE RIBA JOURNAL SUSTAINABILITY AWARD

2000   Chetwood Associates, Sainsbury's,
Greenwich

2001   Michael Hopkins & Partners, Jubilee Campus,
Nottingham University

2002   Cottrell + Vermeulen, Cardboard Building,
Westborough School, Westcliff-on-Sea

2003   Bill Dunster Architects, BedZED, Wallington

2004   Sarah Wigglesworth Architects, Stock Orchard
Street, London

2005   Associated Architects, Cobtun House,
Worcester

THE STEPHEN LAWRENCE PRIZE

1998   Ian Ritchie Architects, Terrasson Cultural
Greenhouse, France

1999   Munkenbeck + Marshall Architects, Sculpture
Gallery, Roche Court, Salisbury

2000   Softroom Architects, Kielder Belvedere

2001   Richard Rose-Casemore, Hatherley Studio,
Winchester

2002   Cottrell + Vermeulen, Cardboard Building,
Westborough School, Westcliff-on-Sea

SPONSORS

 The RIBA is grateful to all the sponsors who make the Awards possible, in particular *The Architects' Journal*, published by EMAP, the main sponsors, who provide the money for the RIBA Stirling Prize and its judging costs. *The Architects' Journal* has been promoting good architecture since 1895. Its weekly news coverage, comprehensive building studies, in-depth technical and practice features and incisive commentary make it the UK's leading architectural magazine, whose authoritative voice has informed generations of architects. The *AJ* also generously supports the Manser Medal.

The RIBA would also like to thank the other sponsors of the Special Awards:
The Centre for Accessible Environments and Nicholls & Clarke, joint sponsors of the RIBA Inclusive Design Award. The Centre for Accessible Environments is an information provider and a forum for collaborative dialogue between providers and users on how the built environment can best be made or modified to achieve inclusion by design. The Nicholls & Clarke Group, established in 1875, is one of the UK's leading independent suppliers of building materials, with a division specializing in the design, manufacture and supply of access products for the disability and elderly care markets.

Arts Council England, which has sponsored The RIBA Client of the Year from its inception in 1998. Arts Council England is the national development agency for the arts in England, distributing public money from government and the National Lottery. The Arts Council works to get more art to more people in more places by developing and promoting the arts, acting as an independent body at arm's length from government.

The Marco Goldschmied Foundation, established by RIBA past president Marco Goldschmied, has sponsored the £15,000 Stephen Lawrence Prize (£5000 to the winner and £10,000 for an architectural bursary) since it was established in 1998 in memory of the murdered black teenager who aspired to be an architect. Marco Goldschmied's foundation also supports the Stephen Lawrence Charitable Trust and in particular its bursary programme which aims to increase the number of architects from black and minority ethnic communities. www.stephenlawrence.org.uk

The Crown Estate, sponsors of The Crown Estate Conservation Award, first presented in 1998, manages a large and uniquely diverse portfolio of land and buildings across the UK. One of its primary concerns is to make historic buildings suitable for today's users.

English Partnerships, sponsor of the RIBA Sustainability Award, is the national regeneration agency that is helping the government to support high-quality sustainable growth in England.

Marley, manufacturer of tiles, slates and cladding systems, which supports the Lubetkin Prize through a generous endowment given in 1988 to the RIBA to be spent on awards.

All RIBA Award winners receive a lead plaque, produced and donated by the Lead Sheet Association, to be placed on the building. The LSA is the primary independent body involved in the promotion and development of the use of rolled-lead sheet. It offers authoritative technical advice and comprehensive training services to ensure that rolled-lead sheet maintains its matchless reputation as one of the most established, long-lasting and environmentally friendly construction materials. The LSA is proud to have been associated with the RIBA Awards since 1989.

The RIBA would also like to thank the sponsors of the RIBA Stirling Prize Dinner:
Autodesk revolutionized the software industry with AutoCAD®. It is a fully diversified software company that provides targeted solutions for creating, managing and sharing digital assets.
With more than fifteen years' distinguished service, SIV Architectural Career Management is the industry's pre-eminent recruitment resource, providing introductions and placements for architecture's most talented individuals and top-performing clients.
As a leader in the industry and a pioneer of new technologies in the UK, Hobs Reprographics plc has been providing services to architects and the construction industry since 1969. The RIBA is very grateful to Hobs for producing all of the print for the Stirling Prize Dinner and Exhibition.
Aram is London's premier contemporary furniture and lighting store, who kindly supplied the Le Corbusier-designed furniture for the Stirling presentation.

The RIBA would like to thank Channel 4 for its continuing coverage of the RIBA Stirling Prize in association with *The Architects' Journal*, and Kevin McCloud and TalkbackTHAMES for their informative and stylish delivery.

PHOTOGRAPHS The RIBA would also like to thank those photographers – whose work is published in this book and who are credited in the main text – who agreed to waive copyright fees for reproduction by the RIBA of their work in connection with the promotion of the RIBA Awards.

INDEX